Alfred Conkling

The Powers of the Executive Departmen

Of the Government of the United States, and the Political Institutions....

Alfred Conkling

The Powers of the Executive Departmen
Of the Government of the United States, and the Political Institutions....

ISBN/EAN: 9783337133351

Printed in Europe, USA, Canada, Australia, Japan

Cover: Foto ©Suzi / pixelio.de

More available books at **www.hansebooks.com**

THE POWERS

OF THE

EXECUTIVE DEPARTMENT

OF THE

GOVERNMENT OF THE UNITED STATES,

AND THE

POLITICAL INSTITUTIONS

AND

CONSTITUTIONAL LAW

OF THE

UNITED STATES.

By ALFRED CONKLING.

"Better to be awakened by the alarm-bell than to perish in the flames."—BURKE.

ALBANY, N. Y.:
WEARE C. LITTLE & CO.,
LAW BOOKSELLERS AND PUBLISHERS,
1882.

CONTENTS.

EXECUTIVE POWER.

THE unparalled struggle, for the maintenance of the Union, from which we have
so lately emerged, is rightly regarded as
one of those great historic events which
shape the destinies of nations. Some of
its fruits are already palpable to the gross-
est sense. It has freed us from the curse
and opprobrium of legalized human bondage ; it has demonstrated our capacity for
successful warfare, upon a grand scale, on
land and sea ; and in proving to us, as it
has incontestably done, that we have nothing to expect from the good-will, little
from the honesty, and still less from the
magnanimity of two, at least, of the most

powerful nations of the old world ; it has also taught both them and us that, so long as we are true to ourselves, we have little to fear from their enmity. It has aroused into unwonted activity all the intellectual, moral, and impulsive energies of the American mind ; and if it has brought out, in bold and revolting relief, all that is most odious and humiliating in man, it has expanded and invigorated all that inspires him with noble thoughts and high aspirations, and all else that exalts him to a rank in the scale of being, "but a little lower than the angels ;" and whatever else may befall us, we may confidently hope that the grand impulse it has thus imparted to our career of intellectual and moral civilization, is destined to endure. Let this great boon be our consolation for the terrible sacrifices it has cost us. But it is not upon these topics that I design to dwell, and I address

myself at once to the task I have undertaken.

One of the consequences of the Rebellion
has been to awaken public attention more
strongly than it had yet been, to a great
problem of constitutional law ; a problem
of transcendent importance, and demand-
ing the earnest and dispassionate consideration of the American people. It was
discussed in the constitutional convention ;
by the contemporaneous public press; by the
writers of the " Federalist," two of whom
were among the most distinguished members of the convention, after it had been
submitted to the people for ratification ;
and in the conventions of the several
States ; and it has, to a greater or less
extent, incidentally provoked discussion
under nearly every administration of the
national government, from that of Washington inclusive, down to the present day.

It has also been briefly treated by our writers on constitutional jurisprudence; and, with regard to ·some of its elements, subjected also to judicial scrutiny. And yet, now, under all the lights thus shed upon it, after the lapse of three-quarters of a century, it not only remains practically unsolved, but presents itself under new and alarming phases. I hardly need to say that I refer to the scope of EXECUTIVE POWER in our national system of government, and, incidentially, to the line which separates it from the legislative power. The subject already occupies no inconsiderable share of the public attention, and has awakened, in no slight degree, the solicitude of thoughtful men. It would have been strange, and, to the enlightened patriot, disheartening, had it been otherwise. Unfortunately, it has now become complicated with party politics, and consequently obscured in the

popular mind, by the blind passions of
party zeal. A hasty glance over the recent
past will suffice to show how all this has
happened, and is essential to my design.
The sudden surrender of the rebel armies
placed the country in a predicament de-
manding, on the part of the government,
the utmost circumspection, the most upright
intentions and the most consummate skill.
The simultaneous assassination of the President added to the perplexity inseparable
from the emergency. That, in anticipation
of its occurrence, President LINCOLN had
profoundly meditated its exigencies, is
not to be doubted. During four event-
ful and harrassing years, in the loyal as
well as in the rebellious States, and in
both houses of Congress, he had constantly been the object of wanton obloquy
and insulting vituperation; but he was
too profoundly sensible of the momentous

responsibilities of his office, to allow his
equanimity to be disturbed by these asper-
sions ; and calmly pursuing the even
tenor of his way, in the conscientious
and faithful discharge of his duty, he
suffered them to pass by him as the idle
wind. Conscious of his own rectitude,
and not wanting in a just confidence in
his own judgment, he was no egotist,
and did not imagine that he was wiser
than all other men. He had read the
Constitution too carefully, and understood
it too well, not to see that the august
political fabric, shaken to its foundation,
and which he had sworn, to the best of
his ability, to preserve, protect and defend,
could be constitutionally restored and reno-
vated only by the joint agency of the
legislature prescribing the means, and of
the executive faithfully carrying them
into effect ; and neither flattery, nor

evil counsel, nor ambition could have seduced him to attempt the herculean task of reconstruction alone, by the assumption of powers that did not belong to him. Had he lived, therefore, but a few weeks longer, it may safely be presumed that he would have gladly availed himself, as he had done at the outbreak of the rebellion, of his constitutional right to convene the legislative council of the nation, to deliberate and decide upon the momentus questions to be determined. His untimely death was inevitably followed by the instantaneous substitution of a successor, in nearly every element of character his opposite. Whether, and to what extent, his foul assassination—a deed destined, by its atrocity, to eternal infamy and execration —is attributable to a deliberately formed hope that the change would be a boon to the already prostrate foes of the Union, or is to be ascribed to the uncalculating impulses of hatred and rage, must as yet be left to conjecture. But one of its fruits has been to force upon the anxious attention of all those who justly estimate the value of our political institutions, and feel the importance of preserving them as they were framed and handed down to us by the fathers of the Republic, the interesting problem I have mentioned. How it has happened to be drawn into the vortex of party warfare remains to be briefly narrated.

When the framers of the Constitution, and the American people in adopting it, deemed it wise, for greater safety, to invest the president with power, "on extraordinary occasions," to convene Congress, the wildest imagination could not have prefigured an occasion more extraordinary than that of the condition of the country at the accession of Mr. JOHNSON. But, for reasons which I abstain from any attempt to unfold, he saw fit, like a daring mariner, sailing forth, without chart or compass, upon an unknown sea, to assume the high and perilous responsibility of dealing with it alone! The country, wearied with the war and rejoiced at its termination; already grown familiar, during its continuance, with the unavoidable exercise by the executive of unusual powers; sensible of the novelty and perplexity of its situation; and half confounded by the audacity of the undertaking, looked on in apprehensive silence. Some alarm was created, at the outset, by the frequency and vehemence of the president's threats of punishment against the now prostrate rebels; but all fears on this score soon gave way to others still more alarming, awakened by the sudden and almost boundless display of clemency on his part, and by the new-born

1*

and growing favor and confidence with
which he began to be universally regarded
throughout the South, and by its friends
and advocates elsewhere. What has
since come to be familiarly called "The
President's Policy," was soon developed.
Throught the loyal States there was an
earnest and universal desire to see the
insurgent States restored to their original
place in the glorious Union they had,
through four years of bloody strife, done
their utmost to destroy, as soon as it could
be done with safety. This was due to the
deluded millions of the South, and especially to those who, at the peril of life, had
remained loyal to the Union ; it was for
this that the war had been prosecuted at
a cost which baffles calculation, and tasks
imagination. How, with a just regard to
the impressive lessons of the past, this
could be accomplished, was the great prob-

lem to be solved. A more perplexing, a
more pregnent, a more momentous question never taxed the ingenuity of man. It
was not a question to be decided by men
who were impatient for the restoration of
the seceded states, as a means, by their
co-operation, of regaining political ascendency, regardless of all other consequences ;
nor by men who had devoted their worth-
less lives to partisan warfare, however
notorious they might have become for their
skill in devices to carry an election ; nor
by a man of undisciplined and ill-balanced
mind, constantly liable to be swayed by
passions strong by nature, and rendered
stronger by habitual indulgence, however
intelligent and patriotic. Involving the
peace, prosperity and happiness of count-
less millions of our race on this continent,
to say nothing of the influence of our
example in other countries, it demanded

the deliberate exercise of all the intellectual and moral faculties of the human
mind, enlightened by culture and reflection. To the mind of the president the
subject naturally presented itself under an
aspect far less imposing. Animated by
the prevailing desire for reconstruction;
favored by the long recess of Congress;
coveting, perhaps, the glory of the achievement, and possibly not insensible to the
allurements of a less elevated ambition, he
resolved, like ALEXANDER, to cut the Gor-
dian knot, and overlooking or disregarding
the lurking dangers of the enterprise, to
advance at once, by the shortest and
easiest road, to its accomplishment. He
accordingly proceeded without delay to
issue an order, bearing date the 29th of
April, for the restoration of commercial
intercourse with the people of the insurrectionary States; and also, under the same

date, a proclamation of amnesty and pardon to all who had participated in the rebellion, with the exception of certain classes of persons, who, it was provided, might nevertheless make special application for pardon.

But the most significant and important of the series of acts following each other, in rapid succession, from the executive department, were the measures resorted to for the reëstablishment of State governments in subordination to the Constitution, in place of the pseudo State organizations under the Constitution of the Confederate States. Assuming that this could not be done without the aid and sanction of the *national government*, the president seems to have had as little doubt of *his* authority to do whatever the exigency of the case required. He commenced the work by an order dated May 9th, "to reëstablish the authority of

the United States, and execute the laws
within the geographical limits known as the
State of Virginia." This order declares
void all acts of the insurrectionary government within the designated limits, and
cautions all persons against acknowledging
its authority, under pain of being held to be
in rebellion against the United States ; and
after various directions to the heads of the
executive departments, and to the judge of
the district court, for the purpose of putting
into execution the laws of the United States,
it concludes as follows : " that to carry into
effect the guaranty of the Federal Constitution of a republican form of State government, and afford the advantage and security
of domestic laws, as well as to complete the
reëstablishment of the authority of the laws
of the United States, and the full and complete restoration of peace within the limits
aforesaid, FRANCIS H. PIERPONT, Governor

of the State of Virginia, will be aided by
the Federal Government so far as may be
necessary in the lawful measures he may
take for the extension and administration
of the State government throughout the
geographical limits of said State." It will
be seen that, in relation to Virginia, the
President availed himself of a State organization already in existence. It was the
work of a convention composed of loyalists
that assembled at Alexandria the year
before, April, 1864. Its history. into which,
however, it is unnecessary to enter, would
show it to be entitled to little confidence ;
but it served, nevertheless, as a pretext
under presidential patronage for the election of representatives and senators in the
thirty-ninth Congress, and thus unequivocally to develop " the President's Policy."

In most of the other insurgent States no
such organizations existed, and the presi-

dent lost no time in supplying the defi-
ciency. And for this purpose, he resorted
to the expedient of appointing in each of
them an officer under the title of *Provisional Governor*, charged with the duty of
immediately calling a convention composed
of delegates to be chosen by the loyal inhabitants, for the purpose of altering or
amending the Constitution of the States.
These appointments were made by a series
of successive proclamations following each
other at short intervals, and are understood
to have been, *mutatis mutandis*, in the same
words. The first of the series was that relating to North Carolina, bearing date the
29th of May, 1865, which, it will be remembered, is also the date of the proclamation
of amnesty and pardon. It commences
with a preamble setting forth the views of
executive authority and duty entertained by
the President, and by which he professed to

be governed in resorting to the step he was
taking. The preamble and part of the
first paragraph of the proclamation are in
the following words :

" WHEREAS, The fourth section of the fourth
article of the Constitution of the United States
declares that the United States shall guarantee
to every State in the Union a republican form of
government, and shall protect each of them
against invasion and domestic violence ; and
whereas the President of the United States is, by
the Constitution, made Commander-in-Chief of
the army and navy, as well as chief civil executive officer of the United States, and is bound by
solemn oath faithfully to execute the office of
President of the United States, and *to take care
that the laws be faithfully executed ;** and whereas
the rebellion which has been waged by a portion
of the people of the United States against the
properly constituted authorities of the government thereof, in the most violent and revolting

---

* The words in italics are not in the oath. They are used elsewhere in the Constitution to designate one of the duties it enjoins
upon the President. The italics here, and in all subsequent quo-
tations from the president, are my own.

form, but whose organized and armed forces have now been almost entirely overcome, has, in its revolutionary progress, deprived the people of the State of North Carolina of all civil government; and whereas it becomes necessary and proper to carry out and enforce the obligations of the United States to the people of North Carolina, in securing them in the enjoyment of a republican form of government :

"Now, therefore, in obedience to the high and solemn duties imposed upon *me* by the Constitution of the United States, and for the purpose of enabling the loyal people of said State to organize a State government, whereby justice may be established, domestic tranquillity insured, and loyal citizens protected in all their rights of life, liberty and property, I, ANDREW JOHNSON, President of the United States, and Commander-in-Chief of the army and navy of the United States, do hereby appoint WILLIAM W. HOLDEN Provisional Governor of the State of North Carolina, whose duty it shall be, at the earliest practicable period, to prescribe such rules and regulations as may be necessary and proper for convening a convention, composed of delegates to be chosen by that portion of the people of said State who

are loyal to the United States, and no others, for
the purpose of altering or amending the Constitution thereof; and with authority to exercise,
within the limits of said State, all the powers
necessary and proper to enable such loyal people
of the State of North Carolina to restore said
State to its constitutional relations to the Federal
Government, and to present such a republican
form of State government as will entitle the
State to the guarantee of the United States
therefor, and its people to protection by the
United States against invasion, insurrection and
domestic violence: *Provided*," &c., designating
the qualifications of voters, and of the delegates
to be chosen to form a convention. Then follows
a direction to "the military commander of the
department, and all officers and persons in the
military and naval service," to "aid and assist
the said Provincial Governor in carrying into
effect this proclamation."

Like proclamations were issued for the
States of Mississippi, Georgia, Texas, Ala-
bama, South Carolina, and Florida. Ten-
nessee, Arkansas and Louisiana were omit-

ted ; political organizations spontaneously instituted, deemed by the President sufficient for his purpose, already existing in these States. In pursuance of the duty enjoined upon the Provisional Governors, conventions were held and Constitutions framed, which. however, *were in no one of the States submitted for approval to the people.* In *North Carolina* the convention assumed legislative functions, and among other acts divided the State into congressional districts and provided for the election of members of Congress, which resulted in the choice of persons who had acted a conspicuous part in the civil or military service of the conspirators against the republic. Two persons of the like stamp were also appointed senators. A like result followed in the other States.

The *Georgia* convention was found to be composed exclusively of unpardoned rebels, but the untoward emergency was promptly met by an executive telegram to "send hither the list of members elected to the convention, in order that pardons may be issued."

These conventions, availing themselves of the predicament in which the President had so adventurously placed, and from which they saw how difficult it must be to extricate, himself, did not scruple to disregard and thwart his known wishes and requests. He had urged not only the repeal, but the utter repudiation, *ab initio*, of the ordinances of secession, and the formal repudiation of the debts incurred in prosecuting the rebellion. The *South Carolina* convention refused to comply with either of these demands. The *North Carolina* convention demanded the abrogation of the oath prescribed by the proclamation of amnesty and pardon. The Mississippi

convention took it upon themselves to
reject the pending amendment to the Constitution proposed to the States at the last
preceding session of congress, to complete
and perfect the great work of emanci-
pation, commenced by the memorable
military proclamation of the murdered
President, by the final abolition of human
bondage throughout the Union. In all of
the conventions, except that of North
Carolina, for the ill-concealed purpose of
securing a pretext for a claim upon the
nation to compensate them for their eman-
cipated slaves, slavery was declared to
have been "*destroyed by military power.*"
Had the President been far less self-confi-
dent and sanguine, he must have seen in
these discouraging and grotesque results
the signal failure of his scheme ; and had
he been an impartial observer of their
concomitant incidents he could not have

failed to see that it had proved *worse* than a failure.

The final extinction of the rebellion, and the terrible calamities it had brought upon its votaries, had served to repress the arrogant and presumptuous spirit in which it had its origin, and had found its main aliment, and to inspire a hope in the minds of all humane and patriotic men in the loyal States of a sincere, if not cheerful, acquiescence on the part of the late insurgents, in such reasonable terms of restoration as the outraged nation, through its proper representatives, might see fit to require. But emboldened by the encouragement held out by the "President's Policy," and its eager and ostentatious approval by their numerous partisans in the loyal States, they soon began to display a spirit of insubordination and hostility to the Union, which, unhappily, seem

ever since to have been on the increase,
and which, extending to the lowest grades
of humanity, has naturally led to the per-
petration of many revolting atrocities.

After a constrained recess of nine
months, but before these incidental con
sequences of the presidential policy were
fully developed, and while the country
was still but imperfectly informed concerning its details, Congress assembled in
obedience to the Constitution.

As the president, to the amazement of
the whole civilized world, yielding himself
up to the dominion of passion, has seen
fit, in a long series of violent and most
unseemly public harangues, commencing
with that address to a mob assembled
in front of the presidential mansion, on
the birthday of Washington, to denounce
this Congress as usurpers and public
enemies, to deny their authority and

encourage disobedience to their enact-
ments, it may not be amiss to pause
here a moment, for the purpose of
exhibiting this unprecedented conduct
of the chief magistrate of the nation
in its true light. It was against the
large republican majorities of the two
houses that his denunciations were exclusively hurled. These gentlemen were
elected by the votes of the same great
patriotic party to which Mr. JOHNSON
owed his own elevation. There had been
no manifestation of want of confidence
or dissatisfaction on its part toward its
chosen representatives, while there were
abundant indications to the contrary. The
vituperations heaped upon their heads fell,
therefore, also upon the heads of those
citizens by whose votes both they and
the president himself had been clothed
with power. No congress, composed of

men more distinguished for ability, probity, and noble and generous sentiments, and patriotic devotion to the present and future welfare of the country, had ever assembled within the walls of the capitol. That it comprised many men who, in all the attributes of character that confer a title to public confidence and respect, were Mr. JOHNSON's superiors, no intelligent and candid man will deny. Such were the men whom he has not scrupled thus publicly and wantonly to arraign, insult and vilify.

Reverting now, from this brief digression, to the meeting of Congress, I may safely assume that the republican members, during the long recess, profoundly sensible of the weighty responsibility which must eventually rest upon their shoulders, were watching the proceedings of the President with lively interest and anxious concern.

It was impossible to approve, but they were inclined to be hopeful, and were extremely averse to any controversy with him, and they were determined, if possible, to win him over to co-operation with themselves, in a safer and wiser policy. But, on the other hand, they were alive to the importance of the trust reposed in them, and cherished no thought of shirking the perplexing duties it imposed. Supinely to fold their arms and leave the president to work on, without scrutiny or show of supervison, would have been not only to sleep upon their post in the hour of danger, but to abdicate their place in the government, and to convert it into an autocracy. Such was the temper in which congress assembled. It was the duty of the president, enjoined by the Constitution, to inform them of the condition of the country, and to recommend to their

consideration such measures as he deemed
necessary and expedient. His annual message was accordingly listened to with lively
interest. Touching the great problem of
reconstruction, he informed congress that,
upon his accession to the presidency, the
rebellion having already been effectually
suppressed in all the States where it had
raged, the first question that presented
itself for decision was, whether the territory
within the limits of those States "should
be held as conquered territory, *under
authority emanating from the President as
the head of the army ;*" and after assigning
the reasons which constrained him to reject
that alternative, he had, "gradually and
quietly, and by almost imperceptible steps,
sought to restore the rightful energy of the
general government and of the States."
"To that end," he adds, "Provisional Governors have been appointed for the States,

conventions called, governors elected, legislatures assembled, and senators and representatives chosen to the Congress of the
United States. At the same time the courts
of the United States, as far as could be
done, have been re-opened, so that the laws
of the United States may be enforced
through their agency." * * * * * "I
know very well," he observes, "that this
policy is attended with some risk; that for
its success it requires at least the acquiescence of the States which it concerns;
that it implies an invitation to these States,
by renewing their allegiance to the United
States, to resume their functions as States
in the Union. But it is a risk that *must* be
taken; in the choice of difficulties it is the
smallest risk; and to diminish, and, if
possible, to remove all danger, I have
felt it incumbent on me to assert one
other power of the general government—

the power of pardon." He further informed Congress, that "in order to restore the constitutional relations of States, he had invited them to participate in the high office of amending the Constitution, by ratifying the amendment to abolish slavery ;" and he adds, that "it is not too much to ask of the States which are now resuming their places in the family of the Union, to give this pledge of perpetual loyalty and peace." Then follows this passage :

"The amendment to the Constitution being adopted, *it would remain for the States* whose powers have long been in abeyance, to *resume* their places in the two branches of the national legislature, and thereby complete the work of restoration." And then, with what may appear to the reader a lofty consciousness of courtly condescension, he adds : " Here it is for *you;* fellow-

citizens of the Senate, and for *you*, fel-
low-citizens of the House of Representatives, to judge, *each for yourselves*, of the
elections, returns, and qualifications of your
own members." The power, thus conceded
to the two houses, the reader will observe,
is, in the same terms, expressly conferred
upon them by the Constitution. This reference to it was doubtless designed to smooth
the way to the speedy admission of the
worthy persons who, as we have seen, had
been chosen to represent the people of the
States which, in the language of the message, were then "resuming their place in
the family of the Union;" and, with the
exception of the removal of a formal impedi-
ment to the holding of a circuit court in
Virginia, in order, among other things, that
"the truth" might be "clearly established
and affirmed that treason is a crime," and
"that traitors should be punished and the

offense made infamous," this is the *only* legislative power which, in this unprecedented and most momentous emergency, the president saw fit to invoke! And even this power, when it came to be exercised by congress, he insisted, ought to be confined to limits so narrow as to render it virtually nugatory, for he denied that it afforded any warrant for inquiry into the political condition of the insurgent States, for the purpose of ascertaining whether they were entitled to be represented in Congress, or even whether the elections that had taken place in them were valid.

It soon became evident that a great majority of the two houses were irreconcilably averse to the President's scheme. Their objections to it were numerous and insurmountable. They believed that in concocting and adopting it, he had assumed to play a part that did not pertain to

his office, that his intermeddling had been
without authority, and that the anomalous
proceedings he had set on foot in the States
were not binding on their inhabitants;
that even if they were at liberty to overlook these grave objections, it would be
premature, and to the last degree hazardous and unwise, at once to admit the persons who had been chosen in the States so
lately in open insurrection against the government, to seats in congress; that to allow
these States to resume their original place
in the Union, without additional safeguards
against intolerable evils likely otherwise to
ensue, would be heedlessly and unneccessa-
rily to jeopard all that had been gained
by the suppression of the rebellion; to in-
vite new disasters; and, in short, wantonly
and wickedly to sport with the destinies of
the nation. Congress accordingly determ
ined to institute an original and search-

2*

ing investigation comprising all the elements of the new and perplexing problem, which it was their unavoidable duty to grapple with and to solve. A joint committee was therefore appointed "to inquire into the condition of the States which formed the so-called confederate States of America, and report whether they, or any of them, are entitled to be represented in either house of congress." With unsurpassed industry and impartiality this committee collected a vast mass of information drawn from numberless witnesses, among whom were several who had played a very conspicuous part among the chief actors in the late rebellion.

"The policy of congress" was gradually matured and developed. A bill was passed by the two houses extending, and otherwise modifying, the act passed at the last preceeding session for the relief of freed-

men and refugees. It was returned by
the president on the 19th of February,
without his approval; accompanied by a
message, in which he availed himself of
the opportunity to maintain and fortify
his scheme of reconstruction, and in which,
referring to the termination of the civil
war, he peremptorily denied the right of
congress "to shut out, in time of peace,
any State from the representation to which
it is entitled by the constitution." The
bill was again passed by the House of
Representatives, notwithstanding the President's objections, by the votes of more
than three-fourths of the members present;
but failing to receive the requisite vote in
the Senate, it failed to become a law.
Another bill was passed, entitled "An act
to protect all persons in the United States
in their civil rights, and to furnish the
means of their vindication." This bill met

with a like reception at the hands of the
president, but became a law by the votes
of two-thirds of the members of each house,
notwithstanding his objections. The joint
committee at length made an elaborate and
very able report, in which, without impugn-
ing the president's motives, they point-
edly condemned his proceedings as unwise,
and as unwarranted by the constitution
or the laws of the Union. The report
was accompanied by a proposed amendment to the constitution, which, after an
exhausting discussion in both houses, was
adopted, and submitted to the States for
ratification. It embodies the mildest terms
and conditions on which, in the opinion of congress, it was either just or
safe to reinvest the seceding States with
their lost rights and privileges, as constituent members of the Union. It declares,
in substance, that the dusky millions

who had been our allies in the war,
who had by our act been liberated from
bondage, and to whom the faith of the
nation stood pledged for the full enjoyment
of their freedom, had a just claim to the
formal and authoritative acknowledgment
of their citizenship, and to security against
hostile and oppressive State legislation;
that in those States in which their right to
vote, in common with men of the white
races, should be withheld from them, they
shall not be counted in the apportionment
of representatives in congress: that no
person who, as a member of congress, or of
a State legislature, or as an officer of the
United States, or as an executive or judicial
officer of a State, after having taken the
oath to support the constitution of the
United States, shall have engaged in insurrection or rebellion against the same, shall
be a senator, or representative in congress,

or elector of President and Vice-President, or hold any office, civil or military, under the United States, or any State : that the validity of the public debt of the United States shall not be questioned : that neither the United States nor any State shall assume or pay any debt or obligation incurred in aid of insurrection or rebellion against the United States, or any claim for the loss or emanciption of slaves ; but that all such debts and obligations shall be held illegal and void : and lastly, that congress shall have power to enforce these provisions by appropriate legislation.

Three of the members of the committee withheld their assent from the report, and made a report declaring their approbation of the President's proceedings, and citing two judicial decisions : one by the district judge of Massachusetts, and the other by one of the justices of the supreme court, in support of them. The first of these decisions appears to me entirely sound, with the exception of one of its propositions, which seems, at least, to require qualification. The observation to which I refer is this: "When the United States take possession of a rebel district, they merely vindicate their preexisting title. Under despotic governments, confiscation may be unlimited, but under our government the right of sovereignty over any portion of a State is given and limited by the Constitution, and *will be the same after the war as it was before.*" It is to this last clause that I take exception. That the right of sovereignty will eventually, upon final adjustment, become the same as it was before, is indisputable; and this, I suspect, is all that this learned and able judge designed to be understood to say: but if the proposition is to be considered as implying a denial to the

government of the right to prescribe terms,
as conditions precedent to its recognition of
this change—this return to the status *ante
bellum*—I cannot assent to it. The other
opinion, which seems to the dissentients
"evidently carefully prepared," though
sadly wanting in perspicuity, appears,
however, to be explicit upon this point,
and upon some others also, concerning
which the majority of the committee
arrived at opposite conclusions.

Referring to "the provisional government" that had been "appointed" by the
President in South Carolina, his honor is
represented to have said : "In operation
[virtue ?] of this appointment, a new Constitution had been formed, a governor and legislature elected under it, and *the State placed
in the full enjoyment, or entitled to the full
enjoyment, of all her constitutional rights
and privileges*. The constitutional laws of

the Union were thereby enjoyed and obeyed, and were as authoritative and binding over the people of the State as in any other portion of the country. Indeed, *the moment the rebellion was suppressed*, and the government growing out of it subverted, *the ancient laws resumed their accustomed sway, subject only to the new reorganization by the appointment of the proper officer to give them operation and effect!*"

Considering that the "ancient" constitution of South Carolina, and all its laws having any reference to the ancient Union, had been consigned to the flames, and that the provisional government was not instituted until many months after the rebellion was suppressed, the "operation" ascribed to it by his Honor, in this phenix-like resurrection, must, to ordinary minds seem magical; but hardly more so than the authority he ascribes to the President, in

another part of his opinion, as Commander-in-Chief of the army and navy in
time of peace.

The amendments proposed by the committee meeting with open and determined
hostility from the President and his partisans, who still adhered, with unyielding
pertinacity, to his plan of immediate and
unconditional admission, it became the
rallying-point of the republican party at
the late elections, and has thus received the
emphatic approval of the people.

But the supporters of the president,
comprising the whole democratic party,
which, with great unanimity, had gone
over to his support, and a comparatively
small number of deserters from the Republican ranks, constituted a very large mi-
nority, who not only condemned the proposed amendment, but unanimously and

strenuously defended the president, and applauded all that he had done.

Thus it was that the momentous question of executive power became involved in the mazes of party strife ; and here I gladly terminate this introductory narrative, which, summary as it is, I fear may prove tedious to the reader.

———

THE Constitution of the United States is obviously, and doubtless was intentionally, modeled after that of our English ancestors. It accordingly distributes the powers of government among three distinct departments. Upon this vital point there does not appear to have been any diversity of opinion in the convention by which it was framed. Everything else elicited controversy and earnest discussion ; and among the numerous grave questions which presented themselves for decision, none was found more perplexing than the organization and powers of the executive department. The lessons of history, collectively, were discouraging; and except by the impressive evidence they afforded of the extreme delicacy and difficulty of the task, and of the necessity of a correspondent degree of circumspection, the light they shed upon the subject was dim. It was finally decided that "the executive power" should be "vested in a President of the United States of America," who should "hold his office during the term of four years." This is declared by the first section of the second article of the constitution, and after prescribing the mode of election, the qualifications as to citizenship, age, and length of residence, requisite to eligibility, and regulating the succession in case of the removal, death, resignation or inability; and the compensation of the president; the section concludes by prescribing the form of an oath or affirmation which he shall be required to take before he enters upon the execution of his office, in the following words: "I do solemnly swear (or affirm) that I will faithfully execute the office of president of the United States, and will, to the best of my ability, preserve, protect and defend the Constitution of the United States."

It was decided, also, that the president should "be Commander-in-Chief of the army and navy of the United States, and of the militia of the several States, when called into the actual service of the United States." This is declared by the first subdivision of the second section of the same article, which then proceeds specifically to invest the president with certain powers, and to charge him with certain duties, as follows : "He may require the opinion, in writing, of the principal officer in each of the executive departments, upon any subject relating to the duties of their respective offices ; and he shall have power to grant reprieves and pardons for offenses against the United States, except in cases of impeachment.

"2. He shall have power, by and with the advice and consent of the senate, to make treaties, provided two-thirds of the senators present concur ; and he shall nominate, and by and with the advice and consent of the senate, shall appoint embassadors, other public ministers and consuls, judges of the Supreme Court, and all other officers of the United States whose appointment is not otherwise herein provided for, and which shall be established by law. But congress may, by law, vest the appointment of such inferior officers as they think proper in the president alone, in the courts of law or in the heads of departments.

"3. The president shall have power to fill up all vacancies that may happen during the recess of the senate by granting commissions, which shall expire at the end of their next session."

The third section continues and concludes this enumeration as follows: "He shall from time to time give to the congress such information of the state of the Union, and recommend to their consideration such measures as he shall judge necessary and expedient. He may, on extraordinary occasions, convene both houses, or either of them; and in case of disagreement between them, with respect to the time of adjournment, he may adjourn them to such time as he shall think proper. He shall take care that the laws be faithfully executed, and shall commission all the officers of the United States."

The fourth section ordains that "the president, vice-president, and all civil officers of the United States shall be removed from office on impeachment for or on conviction of treason, bribery, or other high crimes and misdemeanors."

By the first article, organizing the legislative department, the president is vested with a qualified negative upon all bills, and all orders, resolutions or votes (except on a question of adjournment) requiring the concurrence of the two houses. The nature and limits of this power are too well known, under the name of the *veto* power, to require further definition.

Such is the organization of the executive department of the government as established by the organic law. I trust the reader will discern in the sequel, a suffi-

cient apology for my literal transcription
of the whole of this part of it, however
familiar to him it may have already been.

AND now, what I desire in the first
place to bring to his attention, is the
discrimination made in terms, and so studiously adhered to throughout, as altogether
to exclude to supposition or accident
between the POWERS and the DUTIES of the
president. I am not, I frankly acknowl-
edge, aware that this distinction has been
noticed by any other commentater upon
the constitution, whether in writing or in
oral debate; but I deem it so important
that, at the expense of some repetition,
and at the hazard of the imputation of
arrogance, I will endeavor, not only to
establish the truth of my assertion that it is

3

distinctly recognized and unequivocally expressed in the constitution, but to demonstrate its propriety. Let us revert, then, to
the article in question, as given above. It
is unnecessary to observe the order of the
rather illogical arrangement of the several
clauses, and it will be conducive to perspicuity to begin with the second subdivision
of the second section: "He *shall have power*,
by and with the advice and consent of the
senate, to make treaties, provided," &c.;
and then, separated only by a semicolon,
follows this clause; "and he *shall* nominate, and by and with the advice and
consent of the senate, *shall* appoint," &c.
Why this change of phraseology in one
and the same sentence? Evidently, because
the negotation of treaties was to be fortuitous and discretionary; while appointments
to office were matter of certain and absolute
necessity. While, therefore, the language

of the first clause is, so to speak, merely *potential*, that of the second was, unavoidably, *mandatory;* for so it must, of necessity, have been interpreted, even if, like that of the preceding clause, it had, in form, been permissive, for it is only by means of its official organs that a government can be maintained. Let us now attend to the language of the provision for the filling of vacancies. It is the 3d subdivision of the same section. Here we find a repetition of the words employed in conferring the power to make treaties: "The president shall *have power* to fill up all vacancies," &c.

The language is permissive, because it was foreseen that vacancies were likely, from time to time, to occur, which it would be more discreet to leave unfilled until the next session of the senate. The session might be very near at hand; the office might be one of great importance, and might, nevertheless, be temporarily left vacant without serious detriment to the public interests; or, it might arise from the death of a minister in a distant country, to which it would be unwise immediately to dispatch a successor, who might prove unacceptable to the senate. But in addition to the nomination by the president, and the consent of the senate, another act is requisite to render the appointment of officers complete. They could not safely enter upon the execution of their official duties without evidence of their authority, and it was necessary, therefore, to provide for the issuing of commissions; and, this being matter of necessity, the language of command is accordingly again resorted to. The president "*shall* commission all officers of the United States," is the phraseology employed. As with respect to nominations to the senate, so here, it was not sufficient to *empower* the president to commission his appointees, it was necessary to *require* this of him as a duty, for the fulfillment of which he would be responsible. Again, it is ordained that " the president *may* require the opinion, in writing, of the principle officer," &c.; that " he shall *have power* to grant reprieves and pardons ; and that he *may*, on extraordinary occasions, convene both houses or either of them ; and that, in a certain improbable contingency, he "*may* adjourn them." In each of these instances the reason for using the phraseology adopted, is too evident to require elucidation. But then, upon the other hand, it is ordained that the president "*shall*, from time to time, give to congress information of the state of the Union, and *shall* recommend to their consideration such measures as he shall judge necessary and expedient ;"

that "he *shall* receive embassadors and other public ministers;" (that is to say, unless he shall, for some special reason, be of opinion that the minister sent ought not to be received at all;) and lastly, "that he *shall* take care that the laws be faithfully executed." The reason, in all these cases, for employing this mandatory form of expression, is no less obvious. These were, in their nature, absolute duties, depending upon no contingencies, and, as to their performance or omission, subject to no discretion.

Assuming, as the result of this analysis, as I hope I may do, that I have established the fact, and shown the propriety of the distinction on which I insist, I have, in the next place, to observe that, with the exception of the military authority conferred upon the president by constituting him

commander-in-chief, not one of the designated powers, unless, perhaps, the power
of appointment, is *in its nature executive;*
and that, with the exception of the power
of convening congress, the comparatively
unimportant one of requiring the opinions
in writing, of the heads of departments,
and the veto, all of them might, without
inconsistency, have been lodged elsewhere.
And hence arises the important question
whether the designation of the president
as the depositary of "the executive power"
is to be regarded as, itself, a source of
power.

I have a vague recollection of a disserta-
tion in some form, which I cannot recall, on
the powers of the executive, during the administration of president Jackson, in which
powers were claimed for him as derivable from this source. But I have wholly
forgotten the argument in support of this

claim. And, with this exception, if it be one, I have met with no direct discussion on the subject, except in a speech of Mr. WEB- STER in the senate, to which I design more particularly to refer, in the sequel, in treating of the power of removal. He denied to the president, without qualification, any other powers except those specified in the constitution. His designation as the depositary of the executive power, he insisted, is only equivalent, in import, to the designation of congress as the depository of the legislative power, and confers no power at all. It is abundantly noteworthy also, that, as far as I recollect, these specified powers are the only ones asserted and expounded as belonging to the executive department, by the writers of the *Federalist*, whose well-known object it was to induce the people of the several States to accept the constitution as it came from the hands of its framers,

and, to that end, to make it well understood. On the other hand, in the animated
and elaborate discussion which took place
in the first congress, in 1789, on the subject
of the power of removal from office, to
which I shall have occasion also again
to advert, it was argued that the power
of removal was vested, by implication, in
the president, as a part of the executive
power; and a majority of the house of
representatives, including Mr. MADISON,
appear to have concurred in that construction. This construction has, moreover, the
weighty support of that learned and able
jurist, the late Chancellor KENT, in treating
of the power of removal in his Commentaries. With this exception, however, both
he and the late Mr. Justice STORY follow the
example of the *Federalist*, in limiting their
exposition of the powers of the executive to
those specified in the Constitution, as above
3*

enumerated. And in this predicament, as far as I am aware, this great question now stands, and is accordingly open to the freest discussion.

I have already said that the distinction so clearly recognized, and so carefully adhered to in the Constitution, between the *powers* and *duties* of the president, is left unnoticed by all these writers: but it is hardly necessary to add, that in treating of the powers of the executive, they have by no means limited themselves to those which I have classified as such, to the exclusion of the powers *implied* in the *duties* I have designated under that name. On the contrary, they treat of them indiscriminately, and thus, illogically and erroneously, as I think, confound them. It cannot be reasonably supposed that the primary object of the founders of the government, in specifically and peremptorily enjoining duties upon the president, was to confer the powers requisite to their performance ; nor is it probable that they designed to leave these powers to rest upon the ground of inference alone. If not, then we are to look elsewhere for their source. And where else can it be found except in the declaration at the outset, that the executive power should be vested in the president? The theory that this was, in fact, regarded as the source of his executive authority, serves at once to explain the patent and exact discrimination between powers and duties, and to vindicate its propriety and logical necessity; and, as far as I am able to discern, this is the only explanation it admits of. It serves also, I think, to simplify and facilitate the interpretation of this part of the constitution.

The most comprehensive and important of all the duties enjoined upon the presi-

dent is that of seeing that the laws be
faithfully executed. It strictly pertains to
the executive department, and constitutes
its paramount if not sole distinctive civil
function. But is the president to look to
this injunction as the source of his authority to perform the duty? Let us see
whether it may not more reasonably be
deduced from the allotment to him of
the executive power. There certainly is
nothing in the words of the injunction inconsistent with this interpretation; but, on
the contrary, they appear to me to favor it.
The president "is to take care that the
laws be faithfully executed." I see nothing
fanciful in the supposition that this language has reference to the power of appointment, and that it was suggested by the
disposition of that power, which, as we
have seen, is in effect confided to the president. Seeing that, in exercising his exec-

utive functions, he must of necessity act chiefly through the instrumentality of subordinate officers of his own appointment, it was deemed fit expressly to enjoin it upon him to be careful in the selection of these officers, and to *see* that they were faithful in the discharge of their duties. The oath, couched in imposing language, chosen, doubtless for the purpose of rendering it the more solemn and impressive, requires a similar interpretation.

In support of this construction, I think I may fairly invoke the authority of the first congress, and of KENT, in virtue of the decision of the former, concurred in by the latter, that the power of removal from office, concerning which, as we have seen, the constitution is silent, being, in its nature, an executive power, is to be considered as one of the powers confided to the president as the depositary of the executive power—

the question now being, not as to the extent, but as to the existence of such powers. But if one power be traceable to that source, it must comprehend all kindred powers. The omission of any formal discussion of it by the *Federalist*, and by succeeding comment- ators, is not inconsistent with the supposi- tion of their belief in it. It is not to be supposed that the subject never occupied their thoughts, and it may reasonably be concluded that if they had been of opinion that the president was possessed of no such powers, they would have denied their exist- ence. But other reasons may be assigned for their silence. The American people, by their acquaintance with the English consti- tution, and with the organization and operation of the State governments, all of which comprised distinct executive as well as legislative departments, had, before the formation of the constitution, already become familiar with the distinctive nature of executive power. It was not legislative, nor was it judicial. Its function was, not to make or expound the laws, but to execute them.

"The executive," wrote ROGER SHERMAN, from the convention of which he was a member, in answer to a friendly letter from the elder ADAMS objecting to the participation of the senate in the power of appointment to office, "the executive is not to execute its own will, but the will of the legislature declared by the laws."*

This was a fundamental principle of the English constitution, as well as of the American constitution. It was by the persistent assumption of powers without warrant of law that CHARLES I. lost his head, and JAMES II. was driven from his

* Pitkin's History, vol. 2, p. 289.

throne. "The principal duty of the king," says Sir WILLIAM BLACKSTONE, "is to govern his people according to law." "The king," said BRACTON (who wrote under the reign of HENRY III.), "hath also a superior, namely, God, and also the law;" and in his coronation oath, the King of Great Britain solemnly promises to govern the people of his kingdom "according to the statutes in parliament agreed on, and the laws and customs of the same."

The subordination of the executive to the legislative department of the government, then, is a fundamental and indisputable principle. A systematic and persistent disregard of it by the executive would inevitably lead to intolerable confusion and anarchy, and, if patiently submitted to, must soon end in despotism. What at any time, the president is bound or permitted to do, in execution of his executive powers, depends upon the existing laws. To him, not less than to the private citizen, the law is "a rule of conduct prescribed by the supreme power of the state," to which it is his duty to conform. He is not to take it upon himself to supersede the law, or to supply its deficiencies by devices of his own invention, even for the accomplishment of legitimate objects of a nature requiring the agency of the executive ; and still more censurable would it be for him to enter upon the pursuit of objects not committed to his charge by the Constitution or the laws. If, in his opinion, existing laws require amendment, or new laws are needed, he is bound to invoke the interposition of the legislature, instead of usurping it powers.

Upon this theory congress have acted ever since the organization of the government. Among the almost innumerable statutes that, during the seventy-seven intervening years, have been enacted, there are many which in phraseology, sometimes permissive, and sometimes mandatory, call for executive agency. Sometimes the language is, "the president *may*," or, "it *shall be lawful* for the president;" and sometimes it is, "it *shall be the duty* of the president," or "the president *shall*." These statutes, it will be noticed, also, severally clothe the president with new powers, and impose upon him new duties; and this, of itself, moreover, serves to show how vain, as well as useless it would have been to attempt any enumeration of the acts which, as the chief executive magistrate, the president has authority, or is required, to perform: and this may reasonably be supposed to be another reason why commentators have abstained from any attempt at the exposition of this undefined mass of executive power. When the president has done all that the laws require of him, he has done, not only all that he *ought* to do, but all that he *can* do, as the depositary of the executive power, without transcending the bounds of his lawful authority. If he does this, though unintentionally, *his orders afford no protection even to the subordinate agent he employs.* It was so adjudged, in an early case, by the unanimous decision of the Supreme Court of the United States. I refer to the case of *Little* v. *Barreme*, reported in 2 Cranch, 170. As it may be briefly stated, and in a manner perfectly intelligible, even to the unprofessional reader, I do not hesitate to describe it.

The case arose under an act of congress, approved March 12, 1799, entitled "An act further to suspend the commercial intercourse between the United States and France, and the dependencies thereof."

By the 5th section of the act it was enacted, "That it shall be lawful for the President of the United States to give instructions to the commanders of public armed ships of the United States, to stop and examine any ship or vessel of the United States on the high seas, which there may be reason to suspect to be engaged in any traffic or commerce contrary to the true tenor hereof; and if, upon examination, it shall appear that such ship or vessel is bound or sailing *to* any port or place within the territory of the French republic, or her dependencies, contrary to the intent of this act, it shall be the duty of the commander of such public armed vessel to seize every such ship or vessel engaged in such illicit commerce and send the same to the nearest port in the United States." Instructions were accordingly immediately issued by the

secretary of the navy, under the directions of the president, to the commanders
of the public armed vessels of the United
States, and, among others, to the defend-
ant, Captain Barreme. A part of these
instructions were in the following words:
"You are not only to do all that in you
lies to prevent all intercourse, whether
direct or circuitous, between the ports of
the United States and those of France
and her dependencies, in cases where the
vessels or cargoes are apparently, as well
as really, American, and protected by
American papers only; but you are to
be vigilant that vessels or cargoes really
American, but covered by Danish or other
foreign papers, bound to *or from* French
ports, do not escape you."

It will be observed, therefore, that while
the act of congress empowered the president to give instructions to naval com-

manders to seize ships or vessels bound or
sailing *to* any French ports, the instructions
actually given to Captain Barreme directed
the seizure also of vessels bound *from*
French ports. Under these instructions he
captured and brought into port a vessel
bound or sailing *from* a French port; and
the question before the court was whether
he was answerable in damages to the persons who had been subjected to losses by the
capture and detention of the vessel. The
Circuit Court of the United States for the
district of Massachusetts decided that he
was so answerable; and an appeal from this
decision having been taken to the Supreme
Court of the United States, the judgment of
the Circuit Court was unanimously affirmed.
The opinion of the court was pronounced
by Chief-Justice MARSHALL, who, in conclusion, said:

"I confess the first bias of my mind was very strong in favor of the opinion, that though the instructions of the executive could not give a right, they might yet excuse from damages. I was much inclined to think that a distinction ought to be taken between acts of civil and those of military officers ; and between proceedings within the body of the country and those on the high seas. That implicit obedience which military men usually pay to the orders of their superiors, which, indeed, is indispensable to every military system, appeared to me strongly to imply that the principle that those orders, if not to perform a prohibited act, ought to justify the person whose general duty it is to obey them, and who is placed by the laws of his country in a situation which in general requires that he should obey them. I was strongly inclined to think that where, in consequence of orders from the legitimate authority, a vessel is seized within pure intention, the claim of the injured party for damages would be a proper subject of negotiation. But I have been convinced that I was mistaken, and I have receded from this first opinion. I acquiesce in that of my brethren, which is, that the instructions cannot change the nature of the transaction, or legalize an act which, without those instructions, would have been a plain trespass."

This decision was made soon after the organization of the government, and its soundness has never been questioned. On the contrary, the principle on which it is founded has since been repeatedly applied, in this country, as it before had been in England. Its significancy is too obvious to require comment.

The result of this summary view of the executive department, it will be seen, is this: that while, in the distribution of the powers deemed requisite to good government, it was, under various motives of convenience or expediency, and in imitation of the constitution of England, decided to allot to the president certain specified powers which he would not otherwise have possessed, merely as the depositary of the executive power ; and to enjoin upon him

some duties which might consistently have
been otherwise disposed of; and, for greater
safety, some others which properly belonged to the executive department,—the true
source of the president's civil executive
authority is his designation as its depositary. I am no advocate of the amplifica-
tion of executive power. On the contrary,
I fully participate in the general alarm
at the recent assumptions of authority
claimed under that name. But I can see
no reason to apprehend danger from the
construction I have ventured to give to
the second article of the constitution. It
may, at first view, present itself in a differ-
ent light to others, a light which may
even impart a latitudinarian hue to the
executive power; but I am of opinion,
on the contrary, that if established and
enforced, it would prove a safeguard
against the unwarrantable assumption of

4

authority under that name, by furnishing a definite rule by which to determine its true scope. No one can be insensible to the evident importance of such a rule, nor can it be denied that we are as yet without one. The people of Great Britain, as I have already shown, have such a rule, well settled, well understood, and easily applied; and it is precisely that I propose. The king is invested with certain limited and well-defined prerogatives, which he is at liberty to exercise according to his own will and pleasure, subject only to the constitution, laws and customs of his kingdom. Beyond this, his powers and duties are precisely those I have ascribed to the president as the depositary of the executive power charged with the duty of taking care that the laws be faithfully executed. But in this country the notions universally prevalent concern-

ing both the sources and the scope of
executive power are either too vague to
admit of definition, or so contradictory
as to be wholly irreconcilable. Theories,
moreover, have lately, without scruple,
been made to conform to the exigencies
of party strife; and the president, on
account of his line of conduct with
respect to the States lately in rebellion, is
denounced as an usurper, and applauded
as a wise and patriotic statesman.

Let us revert for a moment to the narrative I have given of his pretensions and
his acts, and bring them to the test of the
principles I have endeavored to establish.
He undertook, alone, to bring back the
rebel States into the Union, reinvested with
all their original rights and privileges as
constituent members of it, leaving nothing
to congress except what, under the circumstances, was, as he understood it, but

a nominal power, to be exercised by the two houses separately. But the office of the president is to execute the laws "enacted by the Senate and House of Representatives of the United States of America in congress assembled." Had any law been thus enacted directing or empowering Mr. JOHNSON to take upon himself a task so difficult and moment-ous? So far from it, in consequence of his most reprehensible omission to con-vene congress, no opportunity had been afforded to it of considering the sub-ject at all. In the prosecution of the work he had thus undertaken, he assumed authority, by proclamation, to appoint and invest with large powers officers unknown to the constitution or laws, under the title of Provisional Governor; and to prescribe, and peremptorily dictate, the steps to be taken by the people of the States with

which he has thus unwarrantably undertaken to deal. To say nothing of his want
of authority to act at all, what right had
he to act *thus* without legislative sanction?
But he is entitled to be heard in his own
vindication; and we are not, therefore, to
overlook his exposition of the views of executive authority and duty, by which he
professed to have been guided, as given in
the preamble to his proclamations. The
reader is not likely, I think, to have forgotten that he deduces his power and duty to
act, not from the 2d article of the constitution, relating, as we have seen, to the
executive department of the government,
but from the 4th section of the fourth article, which ordains that "THE UNITED
STATES shall guarantee to every State in
the Union a republican form of government!" Did he suppose himself to be *the
United States?* We are not at liberty to

question his sincerity, but a delusion more
thorough and complete never swayed the
mind of any man since the fall. If the
people of a State should see fit to aban-
don its republican form of government and
establish in the place of it one clearly
unintitled to that name, congress would
be bound to refuse admission to its senators and representatives; and if it should
persist in adhearing to its new form of
government, it would doubtless become
the duty of congress to endeavor to de-
vise some scheme for the purpose of re-
storing the harmony of the Union : and so,
if the people of the State should abolish its
political organization and thus introduce
the reign of anarchy, it would be the
duty of congress to interpose and abate
the nuisance. But what would the executive have to do in such improbable and
"extraordinary" emergencies, except to

aid, in the manner prescribed by the legislature, in executing its declared will?

A few months after his accession to the presidency, Mr. Johnson saw fit to order a quantity of cotton which had belonged to the State of North Carolina, but had been captured by the forces of the Union, in obedience to an act of congress, passed during the first year of the war, to be restored, and the proceeds of other captured cotton of the same State, that had been captured and sold, in pursuance of the same act, to be paid over to the State. And it is stated that he has not scrupled to direct a like disposition of other property to a very large amount, under like circumstances. Whence he supposed himself to have derived his authority to do all this, I am not informed. It seems clear that his power of pardoning offenses against the United States does not warrant it. Pos-

sibly he may have imagined that he
possessed it in virtue of his military power,
the only other source of authority mentioned in his preambles ; and we have seen
that his proclamation for the regeneration
of North Carolina contained an order to
the troops in that department to aid the
provisional governor in executing the
duties required of him.

Bearing in memory that these and all
the other acts I have enumerated, were
done in time of peace, let us, then, in the
next place, take a summary survey of
the powers of the president as commander-
in-chief of the army and navy, and see
whether they afford any warrant for those
acts.

THIS branch of the executive authority
is treated with great brevity by the

Federalist. It is one of the subjects
of comment in two of the numbers
written by General HAMILTON, one of the
least likely of all men to misapprehend
it. In number 69, where he refers to it
incidentally, he says, "It amounts to
nothing more than the supreme command of the military and naval forces,
as first general and admiral of the confederacy; while that of the British king
extends to the declaring of war, and to
the raising and regulating of fleets and
armies; all which, by the Constitution
under consideration, would appertain to
the legislature."

In number 74, where the subject is more
formally introduced, he devotes to it but
a single paragraph, which, as it is short,
I shall need no apology for copying: "The
President of the United States," he observes, "is to be commander-in-chief of
4*

the army and navy of the United States,
and of the militia of the several States,
when called into actual service of the
United States." The propriety of this provision is so evident, and it is, at the same
time, so consonant to the precedents of
the state constitutions in general, that
little need be said to explain or enforce
it. Even those of them which have, in
other respects, coupled the chief magistrate
with a council, have for the most part
concentrated the military authority in him
alone. Of all the cares and concerns of
government, the direction of war pecu-
liarly demands those qualities which dis-
tinguish the exercise of power by a single
hand. The direction of war implies the
direction of the common strength ; and
the power of directing and employing the
common strength forms a usual and
essential part in the definition of the

executive authority. This brevity is imi-
tated by Justice STORY and Chancellor
KENT in their Commentaries. The main
object of all these writers was to show
the propriety of having the chief military
command committed to the hands of a
single person; and that the president,
the highest civil magistrate, charged with
the duty of maintaining the supremacy
of the civil power, was its safest and
fittest depository. And it is abundantly
worthy of remark, that these three able
writers, distinguished for their compre-
hension and perspicacity, concur in treating
the authority of the president derived from
the military position assigned to him, as
important, or even effective, as far, at
least, as the army and navy are concerned, *only in war*. Nor is this at all
surprising. The American people have, at
all times, been irreconcilably averse to

the maintenance of large standing armies and navies in time of peace. Except a few troops to garrison our widely separated forts, and to protect the frontier settlements against Indian depredations, and the Indians against fraud, encroachment and violence from the whites, in pursuance of laws authorizing the employment of troops for these purposes; and a few ships to guard our coasts and enforce respect for our flag in distant seas, we were to have, and, until now, have had, no army or navy when at peace. The power "to make rules for the government and regulation of the land and naval forces" was expressly confided to congress, who alone had also the power "to declare war," "to raise and support armies," and "provide and maintain a navy." It is true that there are emergencies possible in time of peace, to be effectually met only by the employment of military force. But they were provided for by the power given to congress " to provide for calling forth the militia to execute the laws of the Union, suppress insurrections and repel invasions ;" a power exercised by the passage of an act for this purpose in 1792, superseded and repealed by another, passed in 1795, still in force, and fortified by recent amendments. It provides, cautiously and wisely, for each of the contingencies specified in the constitutional grant. The call is to be made by the president. When its purpose is to suppress insurrection against the government of a State, he can act only on the application of its legislature, or, when it cannot be convened, of its executive. When the object is to repel invasion or to suppress resistance to the laws of the United States, by combinations too powerful to be overcome by the civil power, the president is to be gov-

erned by his own discretion. Of the militia
so called forth, the president, as we have
said, is also the commander-in-chief. They
can be kept in the public service only until
the expiration of thirty days after the commencement of the next ensuing session of
congress. It was in virtue of the first
of the above mentioned acts, that General
WASHINGTON, in 1794, called forth 15,000
militiamen from New Jersey, Pennsylvania,
Maryland and Virginia, for the suppression
of a formidable insurrection in the western
counties of Pennsylvania to prevent the execution of the law imposing duties on domestic spirits.* What independent powers,
then in time of peace, remain to the presi-

---

* The immediate command of these troops was confided by
Washington to the Governor of Virginia. It does not appear that
his right thus to delegate his authority as commander-in-chief of
the militia in actual service was then doubted; and, though this
power was questioned during the war with Great Britain, it seems
undeniable, and not likely to be disputed. (2 Pitkin's History,
421.)

dent as commander-in-chief? I leave the
reader to answer the question for himself,
and to consider whether these powers extend to the political reorganization and
restoration to the Union of truant States,
or to the squandering of the property of
the nation. It is true he may find, in the
annals of our brief national existence, a
precedent for a virtual assumption by the
president of the power to declare war, by
means of an order to a military commander to invade the territories of a
neighboring nation with whom we are at
peace ; and another precedent for orders
to a commander to pause, notwithstanding the near approach of winter, upon his
march, over snowy mountains to a distant
region, and to employ his troops in ruth-
lessly forcing upon the people of a territory,
a constitution which they have had no
voice in making, and which they abhor ;

but he will not fail to discern that these were shameful examples of wanton and wicked usurpation; nor, I trust, will he lack the virtue to blush at their atrocity.

As to the ample powers with which the president is armed as generalissimo, in time of war, they are to be sought for in authentic treatises upon the laws of war. They are altogether exceptional and *sui generis;* they are neither increased nor diminished by their association with the civil powers of the executive. Any attempt, by the framers of the Constitution, to define them, would have been preposterous; and no such attempt was accordingly made. The war-making power was confided to congress, and the president was declared commander-in-chief; and there the subject was, of necessity, left.

I propose now briefly to consider some of those powers and duties of the president which are specifically allotted to him by the Constitution ; and, *first*, of THE POWER TO GRANT REPRIEVES AND PARDONS. This power has been supposed to comprehend every species of legal penalty, from the forfeiture of life to the smallest fine ; and to extend as well to fines imposed by courts for contempt, including those inflicted on defaulting jurors, as to those imposed by penal laws.* It has also been held that it may be exercised before as well as after conviction ; and even before indictment, upon an application accompanied by a confession of guilt. It has been supposed, moreover, to warrant, by implication, the commutation of punishment, and the grant of condi-

---

* Opinions of Attorney-General, *passim.*

tional pardons, provided the condition be such that its observance may be enforced, as, for example, enlistment in the navy.* No argument can be necessary to prove the high importance of such a power as this, nor to show the weighty responsibility its possession imposes. The inherent difficulty of executing it wisely, and its peculiar liability to pernicious misuse, may be less evident, and certainly have failed to awaken the degree of attention and jealousy they imperatively demand. It would, in reality, be difficult to name a power, to the proper exercise of which a sound and enlightened judgment, honestly and patiently applied, is more indispensable. Consider for a moment its nature. Lord COKE, in treating of "this high prerogative," as he justly calls it, of the king, observes

* Opinions of Attorney-General, *passim*

that "he is intrusted with it upon especial confidence that he will *spare those only whose case, could it have been foreseen, the law itself may be presumed willing to have excepted out of its general rules*, which the wisdom of man cannot possibly make so perfect as to suit every case." With this assistance from the analytic mind of Lord COKE, I leave the reader to analyze the problem presented for solution, upon an application for pardon ; to note its complexity, and to compute the danger of unavoidable error. What, then, is to be expected from the heedless exercise of "this high prerogative?" Unhappily, we are not without experience upon this point. During the presidency of General TAY-LOR, a man convicted of coining, systematically prosecuted during many months, upon the clearest evidence, obtained by great exertions on the part of the officers of justice ; who, moreover, was shown, upon his trial, to have incurred the guilt of subornation of perjury, in the hope, by that means, to escape punishment, and who, withal, had, for greater safety, assumed the character of a religious zealot, was unconditionally pardoned without inqury, within a month after his conviction! I cite this instance from personal knowledge. I cite another from a very cautiously, as well as very ably conducted newspaper. Referring to the annunciation, from time to time, of pardons granted by President JOHNSON, on convictions for forgeries of the national currency, it was stated in the New York Tribune, that these pardons already numbered *more than twenty !* This was several months ago. Whether the practice was thenceforth continued, or whether the severe and well-merited censures of the editor, of an abuse so enormous and mischievous, served to arrest or check it, I am not informed. These were among the highest and most dangerous crimes known to our laws, crimes which, until lately, in England, subjected the offender to capital punishment. The dullest apprehension can require no prompting to perceive that these presidential acts, instead of being in harmony with the spirit of the laws, were in flagrant conflict, not less with their spirit than their letter. Of the recent prodigal and almost boundless, yet apparently capricious exercise of this power in the grant of pardons for treason, I leave my readers to form their own opinions.

That the power to pardon offenses ought to find a place in our government, few, if any, probably, are disposed to deny.

At the adoption of the Constitution, neither the necessity of the power, nor, *with one exception*, the expediency of vest-ing it in the president, appears to have been questioned. But it was strenuously insisted that, in relation to the crime of *treason*, "the assent of one or both branches of the legislative body" ought to have been required. General HAMILTON, in the 74th number of the *Federalist*, undertook the task of answering this objection. He candidly admits that there are strong reasons for the exception. "As treason," he observes, "is a crime leveled at the immediate being of society, where the laws have once ascertained the guilt of the offender, there seems a fitness in referring the expediency of an act of mercy toward him to the judgment of the legislature. And this ought the rather to be the case, as the supposition of connivance of the chief magistrate ought not to be entirely excluded." But he had undertaken to defend the Constitution as

it came from the hands of its framers, and
he accordingly proceeded, with his wonted
ability, to combat the objection. Whether,
had he lived to the present day, with
faculties unimpaired, the conclusion at
which he arrived would have withstood
the light of our last six years' experience,
may well be doubted.

I PROCEED, in the next place, to consider
the President's POWER OF APPOINTMENT
TO OFFICE. He is, as we have seen, to
nominate, and by and with the advice and
consent of the senate, appoint all officers
of the United States (with a reservation,
however, to congress of power to provide
otherwise for the appointment of inferior
officers) ; and, 2, when vacancies "happen"
during the recess of the senate, he is

empowered to fill them, by granting commissions to expire at the end of the next session. It will be remembered that in enumerating the powers and duties of the president, I classed the nomination, and, with the approbation of the senate, the appointment of officers among his *duties*, and the filling of vacancies during the recess of the senate among his *powers*, and that I assigned the reason for so doing. But inasmuch as it must be conceded that the duty implies the authority to execute it, and the power implies the duty of its exercise when the public interest requires it, it may be asked, is not this distinction rather nominal than real? It would, I think, be a sufficient answer to say that having been recognized, and studiously carried out by the founders of the government, we are bound, in analyzing their work, to regard it as one of its essential elements not to be overlooked. But if I do not greatly err, the distinction is, by no means, devoid of practical importance. On the contrary, I think that inattention to it has contributed in no slight degree to the introduction of the enormous abuses which have grown out of the power of appointment. By habitually contemplating this faculty as a *power granted* to the president, instead of a *stern duty imperatively required*, the American people, from their presidents downward, came at length to regard it in the light of a royal prerogative, which he was at liberty to exercise for his own gratification, with little or no respect to the public welfare. But contemplating it in the light in which it was so carefully placed by our fathers, we are at once freed from a delusion so baseless and pernicious. Looking at it under its true aspect, we discern its true nature.

5

Its obvious purpose serves to define the limits of the power it implies. We see in it only an obligation imposed on the president by the organic law, to seek out and appoint the most suitable persons to fill the offices therein designated, and to be created by the legislative power; we see and feel that it invests its possessor with no right, in exercising it, to look an inch beyond the public weal; and we instinctively revolt at the thought of its prostitution to personal objects. Such, beyond question, were the views, and the only views, entertained of it by the convention, and by our ancestors in accepting the constitution at their hands. If some vague apprehensions of usurpation or abuse found access to the minds of the more wary, they were dismissed as unworthy suspicions. Among all the great patriots of that day who had been thought of as likely to be called to fill the presidential office, there was not one of whom such a suspicion could be harbored for a moment; and the present imparted its hue to the future. Nor should we be in haste to impute want of forecast or blind confidence to our progenitors. It required the lapse of more than forty years to demonstrate the error into which they fell. Until after the close of the administration of the younger ADAMS, no president had lacked the virtue to take the Constitution for his guide, and steadfastly to adhere to it; and if honesty can properly be said to be praiseworthy, the conduct, in this respect, of the first six presidents, was the more so on account of the superaddition to their constitutional powers, by legislative construction, of an almost unlimited power of *removal from office*—a subject to which I propose presently to advert. Recurring, for a moment, to what I have said of the consequences resulting from want of attention to the distinction I have endeavored to establish, I will only add, that the bewildering influence of the false light emanating from this error is clearly traceable in the discussions to which this last-mentioned power has given rise.

But let us now take an observation, and see whither we have drifted during the remaining thirty-seven years of our national existence. In the prosecution of this task I shall have little further occasion to cite the language of the constitution. In narrating the conduct of the successors of Mr. ADAMS with respect to those parts of it with which we are at present concerned, we shall find them to have been so completely ignored that, in our passage along the rugged path we are to tread, the venerable parchment can

serve no other purpose except, in the end,
to mark the fearful extent of our depart-
ure from the principles it inculcates and
enjoins ; and that it might, at the outset,
as well have been sorrowfully rolled up
and reverently laid aside.

As we have seen, the constitution provides for the filling of vacancies that
may *happen* during the recess of the
senate. It is silent as to the power of
removal from office. One of the objections urged against it while pending for
ratification by the people of the several
States, was the participation of the senate
in appointments. The objection was an-
swered in two of the papers of the *Fed-*

eralist. They were written by General
HAMILTON, who, as well as Mr. MADISON
another of its writers, it is well known, was
a member of the constitutional convention. In the seventy-seventh number,
assuming the necessity of the existence in
the government of a power of removal
for notorious incompetency or infidelity,
the writer also assumes, without argument
or apparent doubt, that "the consent of"
the senate "would be necessary to dis-
place as well as to appoint." He doubtless
regarded it as many others have done in
the subsequent discussions to which the
subject has since given rise, as incident to
the power of appointment, and, consequently, as belonging conjointly to the
president and senate. And as one of the
advantages which might be expected to
flow from the co-operation of the senate
in the removal as well as in the appoint-

ment of officers, he mentions the greater stability it would impart to the administration of the government. And he observes, that "where a man, in any station, had given satisfactory evidence of his fitness for it, a new president would be restrained from attempting a change in favor of a person more agreeable to him, by the apprehension that the discountenance of the senate might frustrate the attempt, and bring some degree of discredit upon himself." Such, it may be safely assumed, was the view entertained of the subject in the convention, and by the people; and it is said by Judge STORY to have "had a most material tendency to quiet the just alarms of the overwhelming influence and arbitrary exercise of this prerogative of the executive, which might prove fatal to the independence and freedom of opinion of public officers, as well as to the public liberties of the country."* This interpretation does not appear to have been questioned by any one, except the opponents of the Constitution, by whom the converse was asserted as a reason for rejecting it.† But during the first session of congress, in 1789, a bill was brought into the House of Representatives "to establish an Executive Department, to be denominated the Department of Foreign Affairs" (soon afteward changed to the Department of State), which contained a provision "That whenever" the Secretary "shall be removed from office by the President of the United States, or in any other case of vacancy," &c., designating the person who, during such vacancy, should have the charge and custody of the

---

* 3 Story's Com. on the Const., 390.

† 3 Story's Com. on the Const., 393.

records, &c.* This indirect ascription to the president, of a constitutional power of removal, met with determined opposition, and led to an elaborate discussion. It was argued by its advocates, that this power "belonged to the president; that it *resulted from the nature of the power*, and the convenience and even necessity of its exercise. It was clearly, in its nature, *a part of the executive power*, and was indispensable for a due execution of the laws, and a regular administration of public affairs."† And they expatiated on the evils

---

* 2 Marshall's Life of Washington, Phila. ed., 160; 1 Statutes at Large, 28. This act was approved July 27; and a few days after, an act to establish the Treasury Department was approved, containing a like provision. Chancellor KENT refers to the latter, as that by which the legislative construction was given (1 Kent's Com., 310) Judge STORY'S account is indistinct, and in regard to particulars, unintelligible. (3 Story's Com. on the Const., 393, 394.)

† 2 Story's Com. on the Const., 393.

5*

likely to arise from the denial of it to the president.

Repelling the insinuation that they were deluded by the splendor of the virtues which adorned the character of President WASHINGTON, they asserted that their opinion "was founded on *the structure of the office*. The man in whose favor a majority of the people would unite, to elect him to such an office, had every probability, at least, in favor of his principles. He must be presumed to possess integrity, independence, and high talents. It would be impossible that he should abuse the patronage of the government, or his power of removal, to the base purpose of gratifying a party, or of ministering to his own resentments, or of displacing upright and excellent officers for a mere difference of opinion. The public odium which would attach to such conduct would be a perfect secur-

ity against it. And, in truth, removals
made from such motives, or with a view to
bestow the offices upon dependents or favorites, would be an impeachable offense."*
And these were patriotic and SAGACIOUS
men! If any new evidence were wanting
of the impotency of our struggle to raise
or rend the veil that shrouds the future
from our view, or that, of all sciences, that
of government is the most abstruse, may
we not, by the light of experience, find it
here? Of this house Mr. MADISON was a
member ; and under his strong sense of the
inconveniences which would almost certainly ensue from the want of any power
in the government during the recess of the
senate, to get rid of an unfaithful or a corrupt officer, he gave his deservedly weighty
countenance to the proposed enactment;

---

*3 Story's Com. on the Const., 393.

and, after expressing his concurrence in the
opinion that no serious danger was to be
apprehended of the abuse of the power by
the president, he added : " In the first place
he will be impeachable by this house before
the senate, for such an act of mal-admin-
istration ; for I contend that the wanton
removal of meritorious officers would subject him to impeachment, and removal from
his high trust." The clause affirming the
power of removal in the president was
retained by a vote of thirty-four members
against twenty. In the senate it passed
by the casting vote of the vice-president.*

This enactment, says Chancellor KENT,
"amounted to a legislative construction of
the Constitution, and it has ever since been
acquiesced in and acted upon as of deci-

---

* 3 Story's Com. on the Const., 394 (citing 1 Lloyd's Debates,
503) : 2 Marshall's Life of Washington, Phila. ed., 160-162.

sive authority in the case. It applies
equally to every other officer of government appointed by the president and
senate whose term of duration is not
specially declared." The Chancellor proceeds to justify it on the ground that this
power ought to be regarded as *a part of
the executive authority wholly vested in the
president*, and in which, therefore, the
senate has no right to participate. "The
president," he observes, "is the great
responsible officer for the faithful execution
of the law, and the power of removal was
incidental to that duty, and might often be
required to fulfill it." "This question," he
adds, "has never been made the subject of
judicial discussion; and the construction
given to the Constitution in 1789 has continued to rest on this incidental declaratory
opinion of congress, and the sense and
practice of government since that time.

It may now be considered as firmly and definitely settled, and there is good sense and practical utility in the construction. It is, however, a striking fact in the constitutional history of our government, that a power so transcendent as that is, which places at the disposal of the president alone the tenure of every executive officer appointed by the president and senate, should depend upon inference merely, and should have been gratuitously declared by the first congress in opposition to the high authority of the *Federalist;* and should have been supported or acquiesced in by some of those distinguished men who questioned or denied the power of congress even to incorporate a national bank."* There is great force in the argument of this distinguished jurist, in sup-

---

* 1 Kent's Com., 310.

port of the power in question, as, in its nature, appertaining to the executive department, as well as truth in his reflections upon it. They were written in 1825, during the presidency of Mr. ADAMS. The Constitution had then been in operation thirty-seven years, during which the power had been exercised only for beneficial purposes, unless, as was alleged in a few instances, by Mr. JEFFERSON. It is not at all surprising, therefore, that he should have admitted its existance and maintained its utility. Had his immortal Commentaries been deferred until after the lapse of only four years, with what reluctance he would have yielded to the force of his own argument, may be partially inferred from a brief note in a subsequent edition. He concurs, it will be observed, in the opinion of the first congress, that the consignment by the constitution of the executive power to the president, is, of itself, a source of power, and that the power of removal is derivable from this source, to which I shall have occasion in the sequel more particularly to refer. Mr. WEBSTER, in his speech in the senate, expressed his dissent from the decision of the congress of 1789 ; and his conclusion was but a corollary from his denial to the president of all other than the specified powers ; for while he was constrained to admit the necessity of a power of removal from office, his theory left him no other source from which it could be inferentially deduced, except the power of appointment ; and as this was vested in the president *and senate*, the power of removal could not reside in the president alone, but must belong to him and to the senate conjointly. But, entangled as the question is, with the still unsettled

broader one, whether or not the president
derives authority from his designation as
the depositary of the executive power, it
must be admitted to be involved in no
inconsiderable degree of perplexity. Considering the vast importance of the power
of removal, it is scarcely conceivable that
it was altogether overlooked by the convention, when engaged in regulating the
exercise of the cognate power of appointment; and, supposing it to have been
thought of, however strange it may seem
that it was passed over in silence, we are
under the necessity of endeavoring to
account for the omission, as the only
means of determining to whose hands
it was intended to be confided. If we
concur with Mr. WEBSTER in his interpretation of the declaration of the constitution, that the executive power should
be vested in the president, the conclusion,

as I have already observed, seems almost
inevitable, that this delicate and dangerous
power was considered to belong to the
president and senate conjointly, as an
incident of the power of appointment. If,
on the other hand, we reject this interpretation, we may then consistently award
the power to the president, as one of the
constituent elements of the executive
power. But this construction would still
be open to denial, on the ground, so
strenuously insisted on by Mr. WEBSTER,
that the power of removal naturally be-
longs to the power of appointment, and
ought, therefore, by implication, in the
absence of any constitutional declaration
to the contrary, to be held to accompany
it. Mr. WEBSTER gave utterance to these
opinions in 1835, and he frankly acknowledged that, confident as he then felt of their
soundness, he could not venture to assure

the senate that they might not possibly
have been biased by the unwarrantable
and unforeseen uses to which the power
of removal had recently been perverted.
What his opinion would have been, had it,
like that of the great commentator, been
formed during the golden age of the Republic, he has permitted us to conjecture.
We had then reached the sixth year
of a new, and, on many accounts,
memorable era in our national history,
commencing with the elevation to the
presidency of an unlettered, passionate and
vindicative soldier, little, if at all, accustomed to self-control. For my present
purpose it is sufficient to say that it
was then, for the first time, unblushingly
proclaimed that offices were to be regarded
as "*spoils,*" which "*belonged* to the victor"
in the conflicts of party. Had it been
designed to limit this dogma in practice to

the filling of vacancies accidentally occur-
ring, and officers newly created by law, its
annunciation would, notwithstanding, have
been in direct conflict with the obvious and
indisputable theory of our government—
that offices are trusts created, not for the
benefit of those who are to hold them,
or of their party, but for the public
good ; and are accordingly to be conferred
only on those who, upon impartial inquiry,
appear to be best fitted, by their intelli-
gence and honesty, for the proper discharge of the duties they impose. But
the practice, thus restricted, would have
been too limited to be productive of serious
detriment to the public welfare, and especially as it was not wholly novel, would
probably have been submitted to without
general complaint. But it was but too
evident that no such limits were to
be observed. Offices were no longer to

be regarded as agencies created and to be
exercised for the benefit of the public, but
were to be literally treated as "spoils," to
which the title of the victor was to be ruth-
lessly enforced, not by the legitimate exercise of executive powers, in the manner and
for the purposes contemplated by the founders of the government, but by the wanton
and absolute perversion of these powers to
this new, base and unlawful end. The
impatient victors were not to be constrained
to wait for vacancies to "happen," and then
filled by nomination when the senate was in
session, or by appointment when it was not.
The tremendous power of removal was no
longer to be held in reserve as a safeguard
against official dishonesty or incapacity,
but was to be audaciously prostituted
to the purpose of *creating* vacancies to be
filled by the partisans of the president.
The process was very simple. **No sepa-**

rate act of *removal* was required ; it was
only necessary to *appoint ;* the removal
was accomplished by operation of law.*

No time was lost in carrying out these
false principles to their utmost extent.
Spies and informers lent their assistance
to the work. The old questions—"Is he
honest? Is he capable? were no longer
the test of the propriety of removal, and
were scouted as inapplicable to the new
system. The inquiry now was, Is he a
zealous, devoted and efficient partisan of
the president? Many hundreds of faithful
and meritorious officers were accordingly
displaced during the first year of General

---

* It was said by Mr. WEBSTER, in his speech in the senate
already mentioned, on the subject of the power of removal,
that an office is held to be vacated by the mere *nomination*
of a other person to fill it, although not acted on or rejected
by the senate, and I am not aware that the assertion was
controverted. It seems strange that this should have been
considered other than an inchoate step, in itself ineffectual
until concurred in by the senate.

JACKSON'S administration, to make room
for successors distinguished for their blind
devotion and unscrupulous subserviency to
his party. This policy was actively perse-
vered in until the spoils were all distributed; and its spirit was rigidly adhered
to in the choice of persons to fill casual
vacancies throughout his presidency. For-
tunate for the country would it have been
had it then been discarded forever. But,
unhappily, it was one of those evils
which, left to themselves, are sure to be
perpetuated, and to increase in vitality as
they become more and more inveterate.
Such, accordingly, has been the result in
this instance. Had General JACKSON, at
the outset, been impeached and deposed,
as he undeniably deserved to be, for
this monstrous abuse of his authority, his
election would have proved a boon of
incalculable value to his country. That

it has, in fact, proved an ineffable curse, is, unhappily, no less true. It was the first great downward step in our national career. By the tenfold increase to which it has led, of all the pernicious elements of our party conflicts ; by the ascendency it has given to motives of personal interest, over the dictates of public duty, in all political discussions and in the selection of candidates for office ; by the nefarious means mainly traceable to it, resorted to for the attainment of success in elections, which have thus, at length, come to be regarded as mere scrambles for office ; by the terrible inroads it has made upon the manly independence and patriotic aspirations characteristic of our Saxon blood ; it has, for thirty-six years, been warring upon that public virtue which constitutes the distinctive and most essential principle of republican governments ; and, unless it be

speedily arrested, must end in the overthrow of our own. In corroboration of
what I have said I beg leave to refer the
reader to a very able and impressive report
on "Executive Patronage," made on the
9th of February, 1835, by a committee of
the senate ; and I shall need no apology for
availing myself sparingly of its contents.
After pointing out and dwelling upon the
large and increasing revenue and expendi-
tures of the government, and showing
that the number of public officers holding their places directly or indirectly
from the president, and liable to be dismissed at his pleasure, exceeded 60,000,
the committee proceed to speak of "the
practice so greatly extended, if not for
the first time introduced, of removing from
office persons well qualified, and who have
faithfully performed their duty, in order to
fill their places with those who are recom-
6

mended on the ground that they belong to the party in power;" and they conclude their observations upon this subject as follows: "It is easy to see that the certain, direct and inevitable tendency [of this practice] is to convert the entire body of those in office into corrupt and supple instruments of power, and to raise up a host of hungry, greedy and subservient partisans, ready for every service, however base and corrupt. Where a premium offered for the best means of extending to the utmost the power of patronage; to destroy the love of country, and substitute a spirit of subserviency and man-worship; to encourage vice and discourage virtue; and, in a word, to prepare for the subversion of liberty and the establishment of despotism, no scheme more perfect could be devised." The report concludes in these words: "The disease is daily becoming more aggravated and dangerous, and if it be permitted to progress for a few years longer, with the rapidity with which it has of late advanced, it will soon pass beyond the reach of remedy. This is no party question. Every lover of his country and its institutions, be his party what it may, must see and deplore the rapid growth of patronage, with all its attending evils, and the certain catastrophe which awaits its further progress, if not timely arrested. The question now is, not how, or where, or with whom the danger originated, but how it is to be arrested; not the cause, but the remedy; not how our institutions and liberty have been endangered, but how they are to be restored."

This report gave rise to an animated debate in the senate, and an elaborate speech from Mr. WEBSTER, in which, referring to this abuse, he said: "Sir, we cannot disregard our experience. We cannot shut our eyes upon what is around and upon us. No candid man can deny that a great, a very great change has taken place within a few years, in the practice of the executive government, which has produced a correspondent change in our political condition. No one can deny that office of every kind is now sought with extraordinary avidity, and that the condition, well understood to be attached to every office, high or low, is indiscriminate support of executive measures, and implicit obedience to executive will."

May it not—borrowing the language of the report of the committee—with truth be said, that if a premium were offered for the best description of the present condition of things, no more perfect one could be devised than that given in this brief extract of the political aspect of the country, as it presented itself to the clear and

penetrating vision of this distinguished
statesman, in the sixth year of President
JACKSON's administration? It requires,
however, one additional feature to render
it complete. General JACKSON removed
only those who opposed his election, and
appointed only those who belonged to his
party. The last of his successors has re-
versed this rule: he prescribes the party
which elevated him to power, and bestows
his patronage on those who labored, to the
utmost extent of their ability, for his defeat!
But while, on one hand, it must be conceded that, upon a superficial view, this
additional feature appears to add ugliness
to the portrait, on the other hand, it must
be acknowledged that it not only detracts
from its force in impelling us onward to
destruction, but affords a promise of future
good; for while it tends to temper the
reckless eagerness of office-seeking politi-

cians, by teaching them that they are liable
to be disappointed in their expectations of
reward by the tergiversation of their can-
didate, it adds another incentive to greater
caution in the nomination of men to fill
the two highest officers in the republic.
But the subject is too grave for irony.

What line of conduct, then, with these
momentous and alarming truths staring
us in the face, does it behoove us to
adopt? Shall we ignobly yield ourselves
up to the current, and flounder on to the
dark and oblivious gulf into which, if we
do, it must inevitably and irretrievably
plunge us? Or shall we, by one bold
and decisive effort, while it is yet in our
power, extricate ourselves from this perilous dilemma, and escape a doom so
appalling? Surely there ought to be no
doubt or hesitation upon a point so vital.
But how is the work to be accomplished?

One thing, at least, is clear. No effort,
however determined, to turn and patiently
stem the current, will suffice. We must
get out of it; plant our feet once more
firmly upon *terra firma*, and exterminate
the stream by exterminating the fountain
whence its foul waters are supplied. Here,
dismissing the metaphor, I return to the
stern realities of the case before us. I
have already intimated that the impeachment and deposition of President JACKSON
would not only have proved an antidote to
the pernicious influence of his example,
but an effectual warning to his successors.
Why this measure of justice and expediency was not resorted to, it may well be
supposed, can hardly fail to become a subject of historic inquiry to posterity; but it
is unnecessary now to detain the reader
by any explanation. He will at once concur in the statement that such a step was

rendered impossible by the extraordinary circumstances amid which the high offender happened to stand. No such step was accordingly attempted ; and the power of impeachment, on which so much reliance was placed by the founders of the government, still remains an untried remedy for executive usurpation and misrule. But the report of the committee of the senate, to which I have referred, was accompanied by a bill, the third section of which was in these words: "That in all nominations made by the president to the senate to fill vacancies occasioned by removal from office, the fact of the removal shall be stated to the senate at the same time that the nomination is made, with a statement of the reasons for such removal."

In the speech of Mr. WEBSTER, to which I have referred, he gave his cordial support to the measures recommended by the committee, including the section I have copied; and he took occasion to express, at length, his opinions, which he said were the result of long and careful reflection, concerning the powers of appointment and removal. He dissented from the construction given to the Constitution by the first congress, the power of removal being, in his opinion, naturally and necessarily included in that of appointment; and the latter being conferred on the president *and senate*, he thought the power of removal went along with it, and should have been regarded as a part of it, and exercised by the same hands. And while he admitted that the decision of 1789, acquiesced in and recognized by subsequent laws, ought not to be indirectly questioned, he thought that congress might, if necessity should require it, reverse that decision. But however this might be, he was clearly and decidedly of

6*

opinion that congress possessed ample power to regulate the tenure of office. It was a common exercise of legislative power, and it was not, in this particular, at all restrained or limited by anything in the Constitution, except with regard to judicial officers; "all the rest is left to the discretion of the legislature. Congress may give to officers, which it creates, not judicial, what duration it pleases. When the office is created, and is to be filled, the president is to nominate a person to fill it ; but, when he comes into office, he comes into it upon the conditions and restrictions which the legislature may have attached to it." Congress might, for example, he said, declare that other offices, besides judicial offices, should be held during good behavior; and if the Constitution had been silent with respect to the tenure of the judicial office, congress might have made it

what it is. And is a reasonable check upon
the power of removal anything more than
a regulation of the tenure of office?

As to the regulation prescribed in the
section above quoted, it was "of the gent-
lest kind." It only required the president
to make known to the senate his reasons
for the removals. It might, he thought,
very reasonably have gone farther. It
might, and perhaps it ought, to have prescribed the form of removal; and it might
also, he was of opinion, have declared that
the president should only *suspend* officers,
at pleasure, only until the next meeting of
congress. But he was content with the
slightest degree of restraint sufficient "to
arrest the totally unnecessary, unreason-
able, and dangerous exercise of the power
of removal." The degree of regulation
proposed by the bill, at least, he deemed
necessary; "unless," he added, "we are

willing to submit all these offices to an
absolute and perfectly irresponsible removing power ; a power which, as recently exercised, tends to turn the whole body of
public officers into partisans, dependents,
favorites, sycophants and man-worshipers."
Being of opinion that the proposed qualification, "mild and gentle" as it was,
"would have *some* effect in arresting the
evils" against which it was aimed, he
therefore gave it his support.

Such an act might now be passed, and
would serve the purpose of a palliative.
But it would not eradicate the disease, and,
with a majority of the senate composed of
the partisans of the president, would probably do but little good. The other expedient suggested by Mr. WEBSTER, of passing a new declaratory act asserting the
power of removal in the president and
senate, is obnoxious to strong objections.

One of the lamentable consequences of the prostitution of this power has been, not only, by familiarity, to reconcile the public mind to its abuse, but to enlist a numerous and powerful army of place-hunters and demagogues to regard it with favor, as their main reliance for success in their vocation. From them, therefore, such a law would probably meet only with clamor and denunciation, as an act of legislative usurpation, while by the public at large it would be regarded with comparative indifference. It must be conceded also that, to reflecting and impartial men, it could not fail to appear to be an experiment of very questionable propriety. The declaratory law would itself, at all times, be subject to repeal, and many years of acquiescence would be required to give it indisputable authority. There are, moreover, serious objections, on the score of convenience, to the participation of the senate in the exercise of the power of removal; and if it could be effectually guarded against abuse by the president, he would indubitavly be its fittest depositary. It may be worthy of consideration, therefore, whether it would not be expedient to endeavor to attain this object by means of a constitutional amendment.

The long continuance of the *usurpation*, upon which I have dwelt at so much length, for such it is, uncountenanced by the letter of the Constitution, and sternly forbidden by its spirit may seem to palliate the offense; but it affords no justification, and can by no means be held to neutralize its criminality. It is not like the assumption of a questionable power from good motives and for beneficent ends; the incorporation of the Bank of the United States, or the law declaring government paper a lawful tender, for example, where the acquiescence of the nation may rightly be held a practical sanction and affirmation of the power. Here, to say the least, is a palpable misapplication and wanton abuse of a power, prompted by no justifiable motive, and productive of the most injurious consequences. Nor has it ever received the sanction of the impartial judgment or moral sense of the American people. On the contrary, it has at all times been condemned by enlightened public sentiment. Those who have practiced it have acted with a full knowledge that a day of reckoning might come, and have, therefore acted at their peril. The first great transgressor—who escaped punishment only because he was more powerful than the law—it is but reasonable to conclude, had but a feeble forecast of the magnitude of the injury he was inflicting

on his country : his successors had the light
of experience to guide them, and have
incurred the superadded guilt of setting its
admonitions at naught.

There are other acts of the present
executive on which I have abstained from
commenting, not because they would bear
the test of the principles I have laid down
with respect to the scope of executive
power, but because their conflict with those
principles is too glaring to require elucidation.

It is not to be denied that the confusion
of the public mind concerning the nature
and limits of the executive power, civil and
military, has been increased by the exhibi-
tions of it during the continuance of the
civil war, and, were it not that the president is bound, and is to be presumed, to
understand his powers and duties, at all
times, the present executive might be held

excusable for having, to some extent, participated in this popular delusion. But it is to be remembered that congress, at its extra session called by President Lincoln immediately after the breaking out of the rebellion, took upon itself the general direction of the war, and exercised it throughout, by enacting laws empowering the president to do whatever they deemed to be necessary to suppress the insurrection, and authorizing the measures to which he, in fact, resorted. An examination of these acts will show that most of them, by their very terms, ceased to be operative as soon as the insurgents laid down their arms ; and as these laws afforded no warrant for any acts on the part of the executive which they did not authorize, so, upon the return of peace, they can furnish none for acts which would have been unwarrantable if they had never been enacted. It is true, also, that in the unprecedented situation in which the country was placed by the sudden outbreak of an insurrection so formidable, the American people ought to have been, as they showed themselves in fact to be, at all times disposed and willing to overlook the occasional errors of judgment, and assumptions of questionable powers, by the conscientious and patriotic man who then occupied the executive chair ; but, however difficult and embarrassing the task that, upon the suppression of the insurrection, was undertaken by his successor, he forfeited all claim to forbearance or impunity by unnecessarily and most reprehensibly taking it upon himself without legislative aid and direction.

If an intelligent subject of a despotic government had come among us immediately after his accession to the presidency, ignorant of the organic structure of our political institutions, would he have been likely, during the recess of congress, to discover, from passing events, that our government was less despotic than his own? And if he had remained here long enough to read the message of the president at the opening of the next session of congress, would he not have sought in it, in vain, for the recognition of any right in congress to exercise an effective control over his will in prosecuting his scheme of construction? These are momentous questions; and if they admit of no other than negative answers, it can require no argument to prove that it is high time for a strenuous effort to restore the government, at once and forever, to its constitutional equilibrium.

THE

POLITICAL INSTITUTIONS

AND

CONSTITUTIONAL LAW

OF THE

UNITED STATES.

That the American people are the subjects of two distinct, and, to a great extent,
independent schemes of government; each
having its Legislative, Executive and Judicial Department; each indued with exten-
sive authority indispensable to the public
welfare, and each, in its appropriate sphere,
in constant activity—as a general fact, is
familiar to us all. Next to the superior

freedom we enjoy, it is the great distinctive
characteristic of our system, compared
with the governments of all other nations,
ancient and modern. It ought perhaps to
excite no great wonder, therefore, that, to
Europeans, it should still be, as it always
has been, a stumbling-block and a puzzle.
Indeed, though the line of demarkation
between the national and state governments
is traced by written constitutions, there is
reason to believe, that to the minds of
many of our own countrymen, it is too
shadowy, clearly to mark the limits of
their respective spheres.

A cursory review of the history of our
institutions will, I think, be conducive to
my design, and I hope will be found, in
itself, not altogether devoid of interest.

When our ancestors, by the achievement
of their independence of Great Britain,
became invested with all the powers of

independent self-government, *three* alternatives presented themselves to their choice,
with respect to the disposition of these
powers. The thirteen colonies having
become, potentially, separate and independent republics, they might severally
have assumed that character, both with
regard to each other, and in their attitude
towards other nations: or, secondly, they
might have surrendered their separate
political organization and existence altogether, by merging them in one consoli-
dated national government, invested with
plenary powers: and, lastly, there remained
the alternative of resorting to a medium
between these two extremes, by the surrender, on the part of the states, of por-
tions of their sovereignty sufficient to constitute an efficient national government of
limited powers, but sovereign within its
proper sphere, leaving the states respec-

tively in full possession of all the residue of their powers.

In deciding to adopt the last of these alternatives, the men of that day took upon themselves a task of transcendent difficulty, of the magnitude of which it is not easy, at this day, nor, indeed, except to those most familiar with that epoch of our history, is it possible, to form an adequate conception. That consummate wisdom was displayed in the execution of this task, has long since, with us, passed into a political axiom.

The framers of the constitution, however, as we shall see, were not wholly without the light of experience to guide them in their undertaking.

In 1774, Great Britain still persisting in turning a deaf ear to the prayers and remonstrances of colonists, deputies were appointed by several of the colonies, on

the recommendations of Massachusetts, to
meet in general congress, at Philadelphia,
to deliberate on public affairs, and they
met accordingly in September of that year.
Several highly important resolutions were
passed, and other measures of great signifi-
cance were adopted by this Convention,
implying a lingering hope of reconcilia-
tion, but adapted also to the alternative of
forcible resistance ; and after a brief session, having first recommended a general
congress to convene at the same place in
May, the next year, they terminated their
session. Their proceedings constitute the
first act of the grand tragedy of the
Revolution. The second revolutionary
congress, commencing in 1775, continued
in session until it was superseded by
articles of confederation. The delegates
of which it was composed had been appointed, without limitation to their period

7

of service, by the people of the several
colonies, to "concert, agree upon, direct,
order and prosecute such measures as they
should deem most fit and proper to obtain
redress of American grievances."

Nothing short of a common sense of great
impending danger, and of the necessity of
united and harmonious action, could have
reconciled a people so jealous of their liberties, and composing communities so jealous
of each other, to the delegation of powers
so comprehensive and indefinite. And notwithstanding the ominous aspect of the
times, and the momentous importance of
the interests at stake, so strong was the
aversion of our ancestors to undefined power
that so early as June, 1776, impelled by
this sentiment, and for the purpose also of
giving stability to the confederacy, congress
undertook the task of preparing a formal
instrument defining the nature and condi-

tions of the compact, by designating the powers of congress, and the mutual obligations of the colonies. The inherent difficulty of the undertaking, greatly enhanced as it was, by the necessity of endeavoring, as far as possible, to reconcile discordant interests and prejudices, unavoidably retarded its completion until late in 1777, when, at length, the articles of confederation and perpetual union between the states, as they were styled, was submitted to the state legislatures for examination and approval.

In passing this new ordeal they, nevertheless, encountered an opposition so strenuous and determined, that it was not until 1781 that they were ratified by the last of the thirteen states. This celebrated compact continued until it was superseded by the adoption of the present constitution. Whether it contributed in any degree to the success of our arms and the establishment of our independence, it is not, perhaps, easy to decide. But, defective as it was, it served to preserve the union of the states commencing in the revolutionary government that preceded it, and, happily, also to demonstrate the necessity of a closer and more effective union. That it continued so long, was owing to no belief of its adaptation to render us a great and posperous nation. Its insufficiency had become manifest long before the termination of the war, and became still more conspicuous after the peace. In fact, it was wanting in the essential elements absolutely requisite to insure either domestic concord, or the respect of foreign nations, and such was the opinion entertained of it by all enlightened men. Its defects, glaring as, in the light of experience, they now appear, ought to excite no surprise, nor ought it to diminish our re-

spect for the wisdom of the patriotic men
by whom it was devised. They were aware
of its imperfections. In the circular letter
accompanying its submission to the state
legislatures, they described the proposed
plan of union, as that which, after the
most careful inquiry and the fullest information, was believed to be the best which
could be adapted to the circumstances of
all, and as that alone which afforded any
tolerable prospect of general ratification.
They recommended it to candid review and
dispassionate consideration, under a sense
of the difficulty of combining in one general system the various sentiments and interests of a continent, divided into so many
sovereign and independant communities,
under a conviction of the absolute necessity
of uniting all our counsels, and all our
strength, to maintain and defend our common liberties; and, finally, appealing to

the magnanimity of those to whom they addressed themselves, they exhorted them, while concerned for the prosperity of their own immediate constituents, to rise superior to local attachments incompatible with the safety, happiness and glory of the general confederacy. Such were the views they entertained of the work of their own hands. Its paramount defect, considered as a system of government—an infirmity of itself sufficient speedily to insure either its dissolution from inanition, or its extinction in the rude embrace of civil war— consisted in the absolute want of any provision for insuring obedience to the resolutions of congress, the sole depositary of the authority it conferred. The powers nominally confided to congress comprised most of the great attributes of national sovereignty, and, but for the want of independent power peacefully to carry them into effect, might have proved sufficient. But this power having been withheld, to be exercised, if at all, by the state governments, the resolutions of congress were, in reality, but recommendations to the states ; and when, as often happened, they were disregarded, the only alternatives were submission on the part of congress, or coercion by military force.

Of this radical, pervading and fatal vice the framers of the articles of confederation cannot but have been aware, nor could they be insensible to its dangerous tendency. It had existed in all the confederacies among the Grecian states and in those of modern times, and had invariably been productive of bitter fruits. Of this the distinguished men composing the revolutionary congress were doubtless apprised ; but they knew also how vain it would be to propose to the people of the several states to subject themselves individually to the direct action of any external authority, for it was against what they regarded as the abuse of such authority, by Great Britain, that they were warring and that their passions were enlisted. In repeating an experiment that had so often proved disastrous, reliance was placed on the obvious necessity of some general supervising authority, and on the magnanimity of the state legislatures. The result, as stated by General Washington, in one of his letters, was, "the confederation" became "little more than a shadow without the substance."

There were other grievous faults in the structure of this compact, to which, however, it would be inconsistent with my design more particularly to advert. But had there been no other than the radical defect already specified, that alone, as I have already intimated, would have rendered it necessary to undertake the arduous task of reconstruction, for the purpose of substituting a national government for the American people, in place of a feeble and delusive league among the states. This great work was commenced, or rather the first effective step towards it was taken, by the passage in congress, in February, 1787, of a resolution moved by the New York delegation, under instructions from the legislature of the state, recommending a convention to meet in Philadelphia, on the second Monday of May next, ensuing, "for the purpose of revising the articles of confederation, and reporting to congress, and the several legislatures, such alterations and provisions therein, as shall, when agreed to in congress and confirmed by the states, render the federal constitution adequate to the exigencies of government and the preservation of the Union."

7*

Delegates to form such a convention were
accordingly appointed in all the states except Rhode Island, and assembled at the
time and place designated in the resolution
of congress. I have said that they were
not wholly destitute of the light of experience. They had before them as a warning,
the articles of confederation—*magni nom-
inis umbra*—and their signal failure. Insufficient as they had proved, so jealous
were the states of their separate independence, that it was not as we have seen, until
1781, that their unanimous consent to them
could be obtained. The same distrustful
and apprehensive temper which had so
greatly retarded their ratification, remained
unabated among the people of the states,
and prevailed extensively among the delegates themselves. This added materially
to the complexity of the task before them.
Without this element it would have afforded

ample scope for all the resources of human knowledge and wisdom. But they were well aware of the necessity of adapting their work as far as possible, consistently with its design, to the prejudices of the peo- ple of the several states, lest it should fail of their approval, and anarchy ensue. The great problem at length found its solution in the formation and adoption of the con- stitution of the United States. This is our second grand historic epoch. Under the system of government thus inaugurated, we have passed creditably to our military prowess, through two wars with foreign nations, and have grown in all the material elements of national greatness and renown, with unparalleled rapidity.

The constitution is purely an artificial contrivance.

When, in 1776, the colonies declared themselves free and independent states,

although this, through their representatives, was the joint act of all, yet, strictly
speaking, it was to the colonies individually, as distinct communities, that the memorable declaration referred ; for it was
upon them severally, that the right of self-
government devolved. They had united,
or rather, they had acted in consort, in
sending representatives to the congress by
which the declaration was made, and they
continued so to act, in maintaining this
declaration by force of arms. But they
had no aggregate political existence, and
collectively could exercise no political
power, except by mutual consent and
voluntary co-operation. Hence the constitution necessarily became what it is, unlike
the constitutions of the states, an affirmative grant of enumerated powers. Its
scope is defined by a few great outlines.
Its framers acted wisely in abstaining from

all attempts at minute subdivision. They
were too enlightened not to foresee that
the practical construction of the instrument
as it passed from their hands would give
rise to many controversies touching its
true interpretation ; but they also knew
that this was an inevitable consequence,
and that any attempt to exclude it by
descending to particulars, would, in all
probability, aggravate instead of mitigat-
ing the evil, by multiplying the subjects of
dispute. They felt that they were engaged
in no ephemeral undertaking. They were
laying the foundations of a mighty empire,
which they hoped and believed would endure for ages; and while it was their unquestionable duty to adapt their work to existing exigencies, they deemed it to be no less
obligatory on them to fit it also to the demands, as far as human foresight could
discern them, of a distant and multitudin-

ous posterity. But who could pretend to foresee the particular exigencies of an indefinite future, and to prescribe the particular legislation they might require? It would have been vain to attempt this for a stable and stationary community; for a young, vigorous and ever changing nation of freemen, the attempt would have been preposterous.

The powers confided to the national legislature are those only, in the just exercise of which the whole American people have a common interest; and they are, with few exceptions, necessarily *exclusive.* The executive and judicial powers of the United States, of course, correspond, in point of general scope, with that of the legislative branch.

The restrictions upon the state powers of legislation are threefold, consisting, *first,* of powers *expressly forbidden; second,* of those *expressly declared to be exclusive in congress;* and, *thirdly*, of those which, though neither expressly forbidden to the states, nor expressly declared to be exclusively vested in congress, *are, in their nature exclusive*, and are accordingly to be so considered. A brief enumeration will suffice to illustrate these distinctions :

1. The power to coin money ; to emit bills of credit ; to make anything but gold and silver coin a tender for the payment of debts ; to lay duties or excises on imports or exports, except what may be absolutely necessary for executing state inspection laws ; to lay tonnage duty ; to enter into any agreement, or compact, with another state, or with a foreign power ; to engage in war, or keep troops, or ships of war ; to make any law impairing the obligation of contracts, or to pass *ex post facto* laws, are among the *inhibited* powers.

2. The authority of congress to legislate, in all cases, over districts and places ceded, for national purposes, by the states to the United States, is, *in terms, declared* to be *exclusive.*

3. Among the legislative powers *denied,* by *implication,* to the states, are, the power to regulate commerce ; to establish a uniform rule of naturalization, and uniform laws on the subject of bankruptcies throughout the United States ; and to make laws for rewarding new and useful inventors and discoverers.

4. The power of direct taxation, and that of laying duties or excises on articles not imported, nor designed for exportation, are not comprised within *either* of these classes, and are, accordingly, *concurrent.*

Our ancestors adopted, also, another precaution. They were jealous of their liberties, and experience had made them distrustful of rulers ; and they accordingly saw fit, expressly to enumerate certain powers, by means of which they apprehended the rights of the citizens might otherwise be invaded, and, in express terms, to forbid their exercise by the government they were establishing. Suspension of the writ of *habeas corpus*, unless when, in cases of rebellion or invasion, the public safety may require it ; bills of attainder ; and *ex post facto* laws, are, therefore, prohibited. Treason is defined to consist *only* in levying war against the United States, or in adhering to their enemies, giving them aid and comfort ; and two witnesses to the same overt act of treason, or else a confession in open court, are required to warrant a conviction. Congress are empowered to prescribe the punishment of treason ; but no conviction, or, as it is expressed, no attainder of treason

shall work corruption of blood, or forfeiture, except during the life of the offender.
These provisions were contained in the constitution, as originally framed and adopted.
Others, likewise, designed more effectually
to protect the citizens against oppression
and injustice, were insisted upon by many
of the states at the time of their adoption
of the constitution, and were, without loss
of time, added as amendments.

The constitution concludes by ordaining
that "This constitution, and the laws which
shall be made in pursuance thereof, and all
treaties made under the authority of the
United States, shall be the supreme law of
the land, and the judges in every state
shall be bound thereby, anything in the
constitution or laws of any state, to the contrary notwithstanding." And that "the
senators and representatives before mentioned, and the members of the several

state legislatures, and all executive and judicial officers, both of the United States and of the several states, shall be bound by oath or affirmation to support this constitution ; but no religious test shall ever be required as a qualification to any office or public trust under the United States."

It will readily be seen, therefore, that while the United States are to be considered as, to some extent, a composite state, of which the several states form the constituent elements, yet that, in a larger sense, they constitute one body politic ; and that, although allegiance is due from every American citizen, as well to the state he inhabits as to the nation, yet, that, by no possibility, can any conflict arise between the two obligations. Allegiance to the national government is his paramount duty, from which no state legislature, or state convention, can absolve him, either directly or by attempting to impose obligations, or confer rights, inconsistent with that duty. So evident is this, that we are warranted in concluding, that those who profess to believe the contrary are either insincere, or the dupes of others who know better.

The immense residue of political power, after deducting that delegated to the national government, resides in the people of the several states. It comprises all political power not so delegated, nor denied by the constitution of the United States. It has been primarily exercised in all the states, by the formation of written constitutions, creating representative agencies for its exercise, subject to such regulations and restraints as it has been seen fit to impose.

The powers remaining to the states are enough, one might suppose, to satisfy all reasonable persons. The annual devotion

in this state, of an hundred days to the
exercise of the legislative authority, has
proved hardly sufficient for the purpose;
and an almost innumerable multitude of
state, county and municipal officers, are
incessantly employed in the administration
of the laws. Whether, and if so, in what
sense, the states can properly be denominated *sovereign* states, is a question which
has elicited much controversy, and no inconsiderable amount of sophistry. The
question is, nevertheless, in reality, devoid
of practical importance. To confer this
appellation upon the states, does not add a
cubit to their stature; to withhold it, in no
degree detracts from it. Their actual position in our system, is fixed by organic
laws. That the more important attributes
of sovereignty, belong exclusively to the
Union, is indisputable. Nor can the states
severally be recognized or known as politi-

cal sovereignties by foreign nations. But, on the other hand, to the full extent of the powers they retained, they act independently, and to this extent, therefore, may properly be considered as sovereign. In other words, while they are wanting in the high attributes of independent states, in the generic sense in which the appellation is applied by writers on international law, to designate the civilized nations of the world as distinct bodies politic ; they yet possess a limited domestic sovereignty. What they severally lost by the surrender of their international sovereignty, they have gained an hundred fold, collectively, by becoming a great nation, and by their recognition as such, among the powers of the earth.

Such then, in outline, is the structure of our political institutions as delineated in our organic laws. It has been in operation just seventy-five years. During this period, and especially the first half of it, many questions—all of them important, and many of them of vital importance—have arisen in the state and national courts, depending on the just interpretation of the constitution, and which were finally adjudicated in the Supreme Court of the United States. Being essentially new, little or no light was shed upon them by antecedent decisions, and many of them were questions of great nicety. No man, not deeply versed in our antecedent history, familiar with every part of the constitution, and deeply imbued with its spirit, was qualified to grapple with them. During the infancy and adolescence of the republic, there was no lack of such men, on the bench and at the bar of the Supreme Court. Among these, pre-eminent over all the rest, was John Marshall, who, for 35 years, commencing in January,

1801, filled the office of Chief Justice of the court. If it be true that extraordinary emergencies affecting the destinies of nations, rarely fail to evoke human agencies specially adapted to the occasion—if, in illustration of this fact, we may point to the opportune appearance of Washington at the commencement of our revolutionary struggle, to lead our armies ; and to that of Clinton, to introduce and carry forward the great work of artificial inland navigation ; we may, with equal propriety, adduce also that of Marshall, to undertake the hardly less important and difficult task of expounding the constitution, ascertaining the precise nature and scope of the powers it confers, and thus bringing our duplex political system into harmonious and beneficent operation. Fortunately for the country, his wonderful perspicacity, power of analysis, and precision of judgment, not only led him, with almost unerring certainty, to just conclusions; but, as manifested in his written opinions, were so evident and striking, as to ensure almost universal acquiescense; and thus to establish, one by one, most of the great principles which were to constitute the body of our constitutional law.

By thus giving prominence to this great magistrate, I have no design to disparage his learned and able associates and their successors, and am far from a wish to detract from the merits of his successor in the presidency of the court, who, after devoting himself with unsparing industry to the duties of his high office during thirty years, and rendering invaluable services to his country, has just ceased from his labors. During this long period, many cases have arisen and been decided in his court, depending upon questions of constitutional

8

law, in most of which the judgment of the court was pronounced by him. His opinions evince surpassing ability, and if his mode of reasoning bears a less marked resemblance to a formal mathematical demonstration than that of his predecessor, they were never wanting in perspicuity or logical cogency. But for one untoward act, he would have held a high and undisputed rank among the greatest judges of the land. Constitutional questions, always, during the time of Chief Justice Marshall, and generally since, have been argued by the ablest lawyers of the American bar. In a few instances there have been re-arguments at the request of the court, and in some, of early date, questions which had already been once decided, were, on account of their great importance, again fully argued in cases subsequently arising, and were elaborately re-examined by the court; the

judgment, in all these cases, I think, being
delivered by the Chief Justice. Now, from
this cursory review, is it not manifest that
the reports of the cases it embraces, em-
bodying the results of a process of dialectics
to the last degree exhaustive, have very
high claims upon the earnest attention of
the student? Can it be doubted that, in
addition to their primary design of making
known the doctrines they record, they are
eminently adapted also to the invaluable
purpose of awakening, expanding and in-
vigorating the intellectual faculties—a purpose to which the narrow technicalities
which unavoidably occupy so large a share
of the thoughts of the legal profession, are
by no means well fitted?

In entering upon the study of our constitutional law, and turning to the federal
constitution as the first step to be taken,
the student is apt to be misled in forming

his estimate of the undertaking, by the remarkable brevity of the instrument before him. This characteristic is attributable to the plan upon which it was constructed as already explained. Every clause of it was maturely and anxiously considered, the intention of its framers doubtless being, to exclude from it all unnecessary verbiage. Every clause of it, therefore, is pregnant with meaning. In short, the great objects of solicitude were, first to determine what it ought to contain ; and secondly, to express it with all possible precision and clearness. But all experience demonstrates that no skill or circumspection in the use of our language is proof even against honest doubt or misapprehension, much less against ingenious sophistry. The innumerable controversies touching the construction of legal instruments sufficiently attest this truth. If there is one writing which, above all others, we should naturally expect to find free from obscurity, it is a will disposing of a great estate, and penned by a learned lawyer; and yet, such wills have often been the subject of protracted and ruinous controversy.

With, I think, but one exception, there has been no difficulty in determining the object of any grant of legislative power to the federal government; nor can there be room for doubt as to some of the more obvious and direct means of accomplishing the objects of a specified power. The difficulty generally has been to determine the limits of the power, or, in other words, in discriminating exactly between what might, and what might not, be legitimately done in execution of it. Thus, for example, no one can doubt that in virtue of the power to regulate commerce with foreign nations and among the several states, congress has

authority to provide for the erection of
lighthouses on the sea coast, and on the
shores and islands of our inland waters;
but whether in virtue of that authority, or
of the war power, or the power to establish
post roads, congress could constitutionally
appropriate money for the construction of
roads, and if so, under what conditions,
are questions that have been agitated during the last forty-five years, and which,
even yet, remain unsettled. So, in giving
a practical construction to that clause of
the constitution by which it is ordained
that the judicial power shall extend "to all
cases of admiralty and maritime jurisdiction," the question presented itself, and
gave rise to a vehement and protracted
forensic controversy in the Supreme Court
of the United States, embracing judges as
well as advocates, whether this branch of
jurisdiction could be extended beyond the

narrow limits to which, at the time of the adoption of the constitution, it was confined in England. A similar question, much debated in congress, arose relative to the specified power, notwithstanding the comprehensive generality of its language, to make "uniform laws on the subject of bankruptcy."

Reverting now, for a moment, to the power to regulate commerce, let me add, in further illustration, that the question early arose whether in virtue of this power, congress had the capacity to charter a national bank. The Supreme Court decided that it might be done, on the ground that, from necessity, much must be left to the discretion of congress in the choice of means to carry into effect its specified powers. The power to regulate commerce was conferred for the benefit of commerce. It authorized the use of means adapted to this end. The creation of a national bank was a measure bearing a direct and primary relation to the subject, and congress being reasonably of opinion that it would be conducive to the object of the grant, had a right to adopt it.

The question has lately arisen and been decided in the courts of this state, whether congress has power to make anything but gold and silver coin a lawful tender in the payment of debts. In the existing condition of the country, it was a question of vital interest to the public welfare. Fortunately for the country, it has received an affirmative answer in the Court of Appeals, as well as in the Supreme Court, and these decisions, the result of thorough scrutiny and profound consideration, by judges of great ability, it may reasonably be hoped, will be cheerfully acquiesced in by the country at large.

Though not in strict harmony with my main design, I trust I may be excused for dwelling a little longer upon this case. The power in question it will be remembered, is expressly denied to the states ; and had the question been otherwise definitively determined, it would have followed that in no emergency, however urgent,—in no crisis however alarming, could this power be exercised. But considering the nature of the power, that it is not, *per se*, an unjust power, like that to pass *ex post facto* laws, which, for that reason was expressly forbidden to congress as well as to the states ; and that there was, moreover, little reason to apprehend its abuse by the representatives of a free people, while at the same time, it would have been hazardous to assume that no occasion would ever arise when its exercise would become essential to the salvation of the country ; it is scarcely

8*

to be imagined that the framers of the constitution designed to exclude it from the
grant of powers to the national legislature.
On the contrary, there is strong ground
apparent on the face of the constitution
itself, for the presumption that they believed it to be implied by one or more of
the enumerated powers. Its denial, for
obvious reasons, to the states, proves that
it was not overlooked ; and if it was intended to withhold it also from congress,
why was not its exercise as well as that of
the power to pass *ex post facto* laws, expressly forbidden ? Recent experience had
demonstrated the necessity of this power
to meet the exigencies of great and urgent
emergencies, and it had been invoked by
the revolutionary congress to the full extent
of its ability. Beyond all reasonable doubt
it was believed to be comprehended by the
power to regulate commerce ; to borrow

money ; or to wage war, one or all. It behooves me nevertheless, lest I should be misapprehended, in conclusion, to add, that however well founded this view of the subject may be, it would be insufficient of itself to uphold the power in question, if it could be successfully maintained that the framers of the constitution were mistaken in believing it to have been indirectly given.

The same kind of difficulty has in like manner arisen in determining the limits of the restraints, express or implied, imposed upon the legislation of the states.

The power assumed by some of them to limit and obstruct the right of the creditor to sell the property of his debtor on execution ; in this state, to impose a tax on passengers by sea from foreign countries ; and, in several states, to authorize the erection of bridges over navigable streams, are familiar examples of this. It cannot, then, I think, but be apparent that a mere familiarity with the text of the constitution falls very far short of an adequate knowledge of our constitutional law.

As well might we expect to acquire a thorough acquaintance with human physiology by the examination of a human skeleton. Among the multitude of unforeseen questions to which the constitution has given rise, there doubtless are many which it would have puzzled its framers themselves to decide. In a few instances the interpretations given to it by the writers of the Federalist, two of whom were among the very ablest of its framers, have since been held by the supreme court to be unsound. He, therefore, who would understand the constitution must resort to the full records of its authoritative interpretation.

This survey, brief and very imperfect as it is, I trust has sufficed to convey a true general notion, not only of nature, but also of the extent of this branch of our national jurisprudence. I wish it was in my power to demonstrate the full measure of its importance. To this end let us turn and take a rapid re-survey of the field we have traversed.

Tracing back our nationality to its source, we find it to have had its origin in the free will and common consent of the American people ; and we have seen that the instrument in which that will is embodied, while it defines the functions of the government it creates, also limits and regulates those of the state governments—thereby determining the political relations between the Union and the states. All governmental authority is, in its nature, either legislative, judicial or executive. By this organic

law, this authority is distributed under
these several heads, among separate and
distinct agents, directly or indirectly chosen
by the people. This law is of paramount
obligation, binding no less upon all public
functionaries, whether national or state,
than upon the private citizen. Every official
act, whether legislative, executive or judicial, unauthorized by it, is therefore an act of
usurpation. It is to the federal constitution and that of his own state, that the
citizen is to look for the purpose of ascertaining to what extent his natural rights
may justifiably be subjected to restraint;
and consequently, to ascertain the limits of
the natural liberty that remains to him ; or,
in other words, the sum of the civil liberty
he is entitled to enjoy. And it is upon
these organic laws and the tribunals established under them, that he must depend
for the protection of his rights. The na-

tional and state constitutions may, therefore, without hyperbole, be said to constitute the charter of our liberties; for it is
to them that we are indebted for the advantages we possess over the subjects of despotic power, and the still more unhappy
victims of anarchy.

This truth, unquestionable and obvious
as it seems, when brought to our recollection, is, nevertheless, apt to be overlooked
or forgotten. Accustomed as we have been
all our lives to the uninterrupted enjoyment of our extraordinary privileges, we
are prone to regard them as the indigenous
perennial product of our soil; and, under
this illusion, to become insensible to their
value, and careless of their preservation.
It is true that in acquiring our independence we acquired the right of self-government. So did the English nation, when,
after struggling for centuries against the

tyranny of the crown, they at length dethroned Charles I, by force of arms. But after first trying the experiment of a republican government through a representative house of commons ; and next, submitting to the usurpation of Cromwell, during his life, they resorted, at his death, to the miserable alternative of reinstating the besotted Stuarts, with their absurd dogmas of divine right and passive obedience ; saw their noblest patriots sent to the gibbet and the block, and endured thraldom and national debasement for nearly sixty years. Whether, then, we were to be gainers or losers by the achievement of our independence, depended on the use we should make of our newly acquired power. If our ancestors had failed, as they well nigh did, "to form a more perfect union," and the American people had thus been left united only by the old articles of confederation—the

sickly offspring of our revolutionary struggle, designed primarily to meet its momentous exigencies, but too feeble for its purpose, even while fortified by the pressure
of common danger ; or, if the thirteen states,
instead of uniting under one government,
had separated altogether, or divided themselves into several distinct confederacies—
an alternative which had many advocates ;
it is easy to discern, without stopping to
enumerate the particular consequences
which would probably have ensued, that
the illustrious prize, won by so much toil
and suffering, would have been rendered
worse than nugatory. That prize is embodied in the noble institutions which it
enabled our progenitors to establish, and
under which it is our happiness still to live.
But from their very nature it follows, and
if it did not, there is no lack of significant
warnings to admonish us, that the enlight-

ened vigilance as well as constant agency of the citizen, is indispensable to their beneficence, and even to their enduring vitality. They constitute the nation and each of the states, a Representative Republic; they can be rendered effective, whether for good or for evil, only through representatives directly or indirectly chosen by and responsible to the people. But how can the citizen judge of the qualifications requisite in these agents, or how can he know whether the trust reposed in them has been faithfully executed, if he is ignorant of its nature and extent? This branch of our jurisprudence, is so free from legal technicalities, as to render it a fit subject of study to others than the legal profession, and ought, in my opinion, to be taught in all of our colleges and high schools.

But the American lawyer! With what grace or propriety can any man assume this appellation until he has mastered this great branch of American jurisprudence? Nor are there wanting strictly professional incentives to its study. A reference to reported decisions will show that a considerable portion of them, both in the state and national courts, have turned upon questions of constitutional law. To some of these I have already alluded; and there is another just announced, which it has required eight or nine years, and four arguments to obtain. It affirms the power of the legislature of New York, for the accommodation and safety of some hundreds of thousands of travelers, and for the benefit of a great inland trade, to authorize the erection of a draw bridge across the Hudson river at Albany. It is to be hoped that not many years will suffice to dissipate the narrow prejudices and delusions which have so long retarded the decision. The

principles it determines are of great importance ; an opposite decision would have
been mischievous and deplorable, not to
say humiliating.

Looking only to the object which, with a
few honorable exceptions, seems, with us,
to be regarded as the "chief end of man,"
discarding all motives higher than a desire
to professional emolument ; it would, therefore, be most unwise to neglect the study
of our constitutional law.

It is from the legal profession, moreover,
that nearly all the judicial and most of the
executive offices are filled ; and it is by
lawyers, mainly that our statute laws are
framed, and that legislative bodies are
swayed ; and it is hardly necessary to add,
that no one can be fitted for these employ-
ments without an acquaintance with the
organic laws, in subordination to which he
is bound to act.   Nor does the public voca-

tion of the lawyer end here. Until, by more thorough education, our citizens, in general, shall become better fitted for the task, to whom, if not to the legal profession, are we to look for the defence and maintenance of our constitutional rights, and the preservation of our institutions, by the prompt discernment and fearless exposure of their covert as well as open invasion ? Let those who design to become members of the profession take heed, then, to fit themselves for this high trust.

If, in a disquisition at the present time, mainly upon the frame of the national government, I were to pass in silence over the horrible pending civil war, so wantonly and shamefully waged for its overthrow, the omission might seem unnatural ; and the more so, perhaps, on the account of the novel questions of constitutional law to which it is giving rise. If this calamitous

event were traceable to some radical infirmity inherent in the structure of our institutions ; if experience had at length taught
the unwelcome lesson, that a republican
form of government over domains so exten-
sive and diversified as ours, could only be
maintained by force of arms, our institutions would be no longer worth preserving.
But, happily for us and for the oppressed
of other lands, there is no reason for this
conclusion. The rebellion is attributable
to a cause extrinsic and fortuitous—a cause
existing prior to the formation of the Union
—a cause, most fortunately, which, though
interwoven with the social system in the
insurgent states, so extensively and inti-
mately as to form its distinguishing characteristic, is yet susceptible of removal and
likely soon to become extinct. I shall
readily be understood as referring to negro
slavery. To enumerate and portray its

diversified, but constantly converging in-
fluences, and follow them out to their
culmination in a treasonable insurrection
against the Union, would far transcend
the limits I am bound to observe. Suffice
it to say that the spirit by which our assail-
ants are actuated—the same spirit that animated Cataline and his companions in con-
spiring against the liberties of Rome, and
that, according to Milton, impelled Lucifer
and his associates to wage war against the
Most High, is the legitimate offspring of
the cause I have mentioned. This result,
sooner or later, was inevitable. To en-
counter it, with all its terrible responsibilities, has fallen to the lot of the loyalists of
our day. How the struggle is to terminate
we are even yet unable certainly to foresee ;
but terminate as it may it will hold a promi-
nent and enduring place among the great
eras recorded in the annals of our race.

On the one hand it holds out a promise of long life, and a career of unexampled prosperity and greatness to the republic, by the defeat of the conspiracy for its overthrow, and by the extinction of its cause. On the other hand it threatens a permanent severance of the Union, to be followed by contention, border violence, standing armies, wars, further disintegration, foreign alliances, and, probably, the final abandonment or suppression of free institutions on this continent. It is the magnitude of the interests at stake, and the well founded dread of these and other evils that make it our paramount duty, at whatever cost, to persist in our efforts to suppress this unhallowed revolt. Even though they should fail, they will at least entitle us to the approval, if not to the applause of future ages ; but if, as we confidently expect, our exertions shall be crowned with success, who can ade-

quately conceive the full measure of grati-
tude that posterity will accord to us? Let
us not repine then at the costly sacrifices,
great as they are, which are required at our
hands. It may be that those of our loyal
countrymen collectively, who were upon
the stage at the breaking out of the rebellion, had they been tame enough supinely
to submit to the insolent demands of the
traitors, would have personally been gainers
by doing so. But let us remember that by
the adoption of this alternative, we should
have justly incurred the contempt and deris-
ion of mankind, forfeited our rank among
the nations, and betrayed our high trust as
the assertors and guardians of the rights of
man. Let us rejoice then that we have
escaped this ignominy. True the great
cause has exacted an innumerable army of
martyrs. So did our revolutionary struggle. There can be no question that our an-

cestors in 1774, when the first revolutionary
congress assembled, would in the same
sense, have been infinite gainers by submitting to a trifling tax unrighteously imposed by the British Parliament, instead of
standing resolutely upon their rights, and
incurring the horrors of a seven years war
waged against them by the most powerful
nation then upon earth. This they well
knew, but they were animated by higher
motives. They scorned to wear chains, and
especially did they disdain to leave them as
a heritage to their children. They were
wise and thoughtful men, and they knew
that life, even to its possessor, derives its
chief value from the power of doing good
to others ; and in deciding to devote their
lives to the cause of human freedom, it
sufficed for them to know that, to borrow
the language of a noble poet,

"They never fail who die
In a great cause; the block may soak their gore;
Their heads may sodden in the sun, their limbs
Be strung to city gates and castle walls!
But still their spirit walks abroad. Though years
Elapse, and others share as dark a doom,
They but augment the deep and sweeping thoughts
Which o'erpower all others, and conduct
The world at last to freedom."

www.ingramcontent.com/pod-product-compliance
Lightning Source LLC
Chambersburg PA
CBHW030835270326
41928CB00007B/1063